T0152086

The Train Driver

AND OTHER PLAYS

The Train Driver

AND OTHER PLAYS

Athol Fugard

THEATRE COMMUNICATIONS GROUP
NEW YORK
2012

The Train Driver and Other Plays is copyright © 2012 by Athol Fugard

The Train Driver, Coming Home and *Have You Seen Us?* are copyright © 2012 by Athol Fugard

Pages from a Notebook is copyright © 2012 by Athol Fugard

Afterword and Glossary are copyright © 2012 by Marianne McDonald

The Train Driver and Other Plays is published by Theatre Communications Group, Inc., 520 Eighth Avenue, 24th Floor, New York, NY 10018-4156

All Rights Reserved. Except for brief passages quoted in newspaper, magazine, radio or television reviews, no part of this book may be reproduced in any form or by any means, electronic or mechanical, including photocopying or recording, or by an information storage and retrieval system, without permission in writing from the publisher.

Professionals and amateurs are hereby warned that this material, being fully protected under the Copyright Laws of the United States of America and all other countries of the Berne and Universal Copyright Conventions, is subject to a royalty. All rights, including but not limited to, professional, amateur, recording, motion picture, recitation, lecturing, public reading, radio and television broadcasting, and the rights of translation into foreign languages are expressly reserved. Particular emphasis is placed on the question of readings and all uses of this book by educational institutions, permission for which must be secured from the author's representative: William Morris Endeavor Entertainment, 1325 Avenue of the Americas, New York, NY 10019, (212) 586-5100.

A version of Pages from a Notebook was published in *Karoo and Other Stories*, David Philip Publishers, South Africa, 2005.

The publication of *The Train Driver and Other Plays* by Athol Fugard, through TCG's Book Program, is made possible in part by the New York State Council on the Arts with the support of Governor Andrew Cuomo and the New York State Legislature.

TCG books are exclusively distributed to the book trade by Consortium Book Sales and Distribution.

Cataloging-in-Publication data is on file at the Library of Congress, Washington, D.C.

eISBN: 978-1-55936-732-5

Book design and composition by Lisa Govan
Cover design by Mark Melnick
Cover photograph by Alex Espinosa / Millennium Images

First Edition, September 2012

Contents

CONTENTS

The Train Driver

For Pumla Lolwana and her three children—
Lindani, Andile and Sesanda—who died on the railway tracks
between Philippi and Nyanga on the Cape Flats
on Friday, December 8, 2000

Production History

The Train Driver received its world premiere at The Fugard Theatre (Eric Abraham, Producer; Mannie Manim, Executive Director; Mark Dornford-May, Artistic Director) in Cape Town, South Africa, on March 24, 2010. The production was directed by the author and Ross Devenish; the designer was Saul Radomsky, the lighting designer was Mannie Manim. The cast was:

SIMON (ANDILE) HANABE	Owen L Sejake
ROELF (RUDOLF) VISAGIE	Sean Taylor

The play received its U.S. premiere at The Fountain Theatre (Deborah Lawlor, Producing Artistic Director; Stephen Sachs, Co-Artistic Director; Simon Levy, Producing Director/Dramaturg) in Los Angeles, in October 2010. The production was directed by Stephen Sachs; the set designer was Jeff McLaughlin, the costume designer was Dana Rebecca Woods, the lighting designer was Ken Booth, the sound designer was David B. Marling, the production stage manager was Elna Kordijan. The cast was:

SIMON (ANDILE) HANABE	Adolphus Ward
ROELF (RUDOLF) VISAGIE	Morlan Higgins

The play opened at the Long Wharf Theatre (Gordon Edelstein, Artistic Director; Ray Cullom, Managing Director) in New Haven, Connecticut, on October 27, 2010. The production was directed by Gordon Edelstein; the set designer was Eugene Lee, the costume designer was Susan Hilferty, the lighting designer was Christopher Akerlind, the sound designer was John Gromada, the stage manager was Cole Bonenberger. The cast was:

SIMON (ANDILE) HANABE	Anthony Chisholm
ROELF (RUDOLF) VISAGIE	Harry Groener

The play opened at Signature Theatre Company (James Houghton, Founding Artistic Director; Erika Malin, Executive Director) in New York, on August 14, 2012. The production was directed by the author; the set designer was Christopher H. Barreca, the costume designer was Susan Hilferty, the lighting designer was Stephen Strawbridge, the sound designer was Brett Jarvis; original music was by Doug Wieselman; the production stage manager was Linda Marvel. The cast was:

SIMON (ANDILE) HANABE	Leon Addison Brown
ROELF (RUDOLF) VISAGIE	Ritchie Coster

Characters

SIMON (ANDILE) HANABE: an old African man; a gravedigger.

ROELF (RUDOLF) VISAGIE: train driver in his late thirties.

Prologue

Simon Hanabe is bareheaded and we can see a lot of gray hair. He holds a little woolen cap in one hand as he talks directly to the audience.

SIMON: My name is Simon Hanabe, I am the one who puts the nameless ones in the grave. This is how it happened. When I first see the whiteman . . . he is walking among the amangcwaba where the ones with names is sleeping. It is the first time I see that whiteman. Sometimes he goes down on the ground and I think he is reading the names but then he stands up and walks some more . . . and looking, looking. All the time he is looking at the ingcwaba. So I say to myself: Simon, what is this man doing here among our sleeping people? Who is he looking for? Then he sees me watching him and he comes to me and starts talking but that time I didn't know what he was saying— his words were all mixed up like he was drunk. So he gets very cross with me when I shake my head and tell him

I don't know what he is saying. So he leaves me and walks around some more. Then I see he gets tired and I feel sorry for him so I go to him and tell him that there is no white people sleeping there where he is looking in Shukuma. Only black people. And he says no, he isn't looking for a white people. He is looking for a black one without a name. So I show him where they are sleeping, the ones without names. There are many amangcwaba here and he asks me do I know who they are and I tell him no, I know who they are because these are the ones without names. And I ask him who he is looking for and he tells me it is umfazi . . . a woman . . . a young woman with a baby on her back. I ask him if the baby is also dead and he says yes the baby is also dead.

(Segue into . . .)

Scene 1

The graveyard of Shukuma, a squatter camp on the outskirts of Port Elizabeth. It is a rocky weed-choked stretch of veld.

The graves are simple mounds of soil packed down with stones. To one side are a few graves, the person buried identified by a simple name board or wooden cross—all weather beaten. Most of the space however is taken up by nameless graves. Most of these have a piece of discarded junk on them: a rusty motorcar hubcap, an empty plastic bottle, etc. The wind has blown away a lot of the soil of some of the graves and, as a result, they now rise only a few inches above the ground. On one side there is a straggling wire fence and on the other a typical squatter camp shack. It is an image of desolate finality.

Standing among the graves and looking around helplessly is an exhausted and distressed Roelf Visagie. It has obviously been a long and hot day—his shirt is unbuttoned and hanging out of his trousers and he is wiping a sweaty neck and chest with a handkerchief.

Watching him at a distance and leaning on a spade is Simon.

The time is late afternoon. In the course of the scene the light fades into twilight.

ATHOL FUGARD

ROELF *(To Simon)*: Mr. Mdoda the undertaker remembers her.
About four weeks ago. He said he brought her to you to
bury.

SIMON *(Going up to Roelf)*: Then she is here. Because this is
where they are, the ones without names. When Mr.
Mdoda bring me the next one, I dig the hole here.

(He indicates a specific spot for the next grave.)

ROELF *(Looking around and shaking his head in mixture of despair
and disbelief)*: Fucking hell! What a miserable bloody ending to your life's story. I wouldn't even bury my dog like
this, man! *(Goes to one grave and picks up an old motorcar
hubcap)* And all this rubbish on the graves? What the hell
is the idea? Hey? Get to Heaven faster with a Jetta hubcap? Look at them all. Who the hell puts all this junk on
the graves?

SIMON: Me.

ROELF: You? *(Walking among the graves and looking at the various
items Simon has placed on them)* You put these here?

SIMON: Ewe. There is no flowers in Shukuma.

ROELF: I see! So that is what it's supposed to be . . . respect for
the dead! Then why not just a simple cross, man! All you
need is two little sticks like that one over there . . . and a
piece of string . . . and then tie them together. *(Crosses his
two forefingers and holds them up for Simon to see)* Remember Jesus? You people are also supposed to believe in God
and Jesus, isn't that so?

SIMON *(Shaking his head)*: Is no good to make cross. People
they come and steal it to make fire to keep warm and cook
food.

ROELF: So now there is also no sticks in Shukuma . . . only
rubbish!

*(A helpless gesture as he slumps to the ground, resting his
back against a fence post)* No . . . I give up. S'trues God . . .

I've had it. This is it. Where the hell do I go from here. Ja! Hell! That is where she deserves to be. I mean . . . Jesus . . . I spent nearly the whole fucking day walking that Swartkops bush trying to find the pondok where she lived or somebody that knew her.

I walked that bush three times—one time with a black policeman from the Motherwell police station and two times by myself. From one miserable bloody pondok to another. And every time I asked them: "Is anybody here missing a woman and a baby?" Sometimes they would ask: "What did she look like?" And I would tell them: "She was a young woman with a red doek on her head, and an old gray blanket that was holding a baby on her back." I know that description off by heart because that is what I saw. Then of course they would just shake their heads and sometimes I could see they wasn't even listening to me. A couple of times they hated me very much and then it was: "Suga wena" or "Voetsek, witman," which was okay because I wanted to say and you fuck off as well . . . and what's more I did. One guy was drunk and asked me if I wanted to fuck a black woman and said he would get me one. It's pathetic, man! Those people live like animals. No toilets, so their places was always stinking of shit, if you will excuse the language—the children crawling around in the dirt with no clothes on. I told one woman to wipe her baby's nose because he was eating his own snot. What made it worse is that I got so deurmekaar on those foot-paths, I would end up at the same pondok two or three times and start asking my questions until they would say, "Why is the baas asking us again?" It was too much for me, man. So then it's back to the police station, who send me to the morgue, and then the old chap there says it's Mr. Mdoda, the undertaker, I must speak to because he always buries the ones without names, and finally Mr. Mdoda sends me here. Here! Look at it.

(He looks around, then gets up and makes one more limp attempt to find the grave of the woman he is looking for.)

And you sure you don't know anyone who is buried here?

SIMON: I tell you, whiteman: this is the place for the ones without names.

ROELF: What about this one. A man or woman? You know . . . amadoda . . . abafazi.

SIMON *(Shocked)*: What you ask, whiteman! I don't open the bag and look. I dig and put them in. It is hard work now. I must dig deep because the dogs come. When I first come here to Shukuma there was no dogs in the bush. Now there is many and they are hungry. They come at night and try to dig them up. *(Picks up a stone on one of the graves)* I put stones now on the graves to throw at them.

(Moves slowly among the graves shoveling a little sand back on to the ones that are on the point of disappearing) And then there is also the wind. When it is strong it blows the sand away. Too much wind! Sometimes it blows one days, two days, three days, four days, and Simon must sit there in his shack all the time and wait. I can't dig because the sand is getting in my eyes.

So why you want this woman with the red doek? Did she work for you in the house?

ROELF: No.

(He slumps down on the ground with his back to the fence post.)

SIMON: Did she do the washing in the backyard?

ROELF: No.

SIMON: Did she steal from you?

ROELF: NO!

SIMON: Then when you find her ingcwaba what you do? You want to dig her up?

ROELF *(Now extremely exasperated by Simon's persistent questions)*:

I want to find her because . . . Okay . . . you want to know why? Then I'll tell you . . . *(He can no longer restrain himself from telling the truth)* Right now, my good friend . . . the way I feel right now is that if you can show me her grave I will stand there, take a nice deep breath, and then I will swear at her until I am blue in the fucking face!

SIMON *(Shocked)*: Curse her?

ROELF: Ja. I want to swear at her until she knows she's a piece of black shit.

SIMON: Dead . . . no name . . . and you want to swear at her?

ROELF *(With vicious deliberation)*: Ja. Give me her name . . . or show me her grave . . . and I will do it. S'trues God. In both official languages because I am fully bilingual. And don't think I am just talking about: "Go to hell!" and "Your mother's cunt!" because I can do a hell of a lot better than that. I'll do it so that her ghost will hear me. I'll tell her how she has fucked up my life . . . the selfish black bitch . . . that I am sitting here with my arse in the dirt because thanks to her I am losing everything . . . my home, my family, my job . . . my bloody mind! Ja! Another fucking day like this one and I won't know who I am anymore or what the fuck I am doing! Jesus! Jesus! Jesus! Help me!

(Roelf cannot contain the emotion that has been building up in him. Now at last it is released in stifled tears and sobs that shake his body. Simon is very disturbed by the other man's behavior and presence. He tries to return to his attempts at tidying up the graves, while at the same time looking around nervously and registering the onset of twilight.)

SIMON *(After a long pause)*: Whiteman! You can't sit here. Just now it is getting dark and then this place is dangerous. If the amagintsa find you they will take out their knives. You don't belong here. You must go.

ROELF: Ama who?

SIMON: Amagintsa. The gangs . . . the young boys. The tsotsi. They won't like you.

ROELF *(Sarcastically)*: Like you do hey! So what you waiting for? Go call them.

SIMON: Be careful. Don't make jokes, whiteman. You must go.

ROELF: Go where? There's nowhere to go from here. This is it. All passengers off please! End of the fucking line. *(Pointing to the graves)* Look at them, for God's sake.

SIMON: They are sleeping now . . . and wena, you are awake. Go to your home!

ROELF: Home? Don't you understand anything. I've crashed! I was on the rails, I was going forward, everything up to schedule . . . until it all crashed. Thanks to that woman with the red doek I don't know if I've got a home anymore. I don't know if I've got a family anymore, or a job or . . . ja . . . a life. You said it: this is the place for the ones without names . . . and I think I'm one of them now. Roelf Visagie? Who the hell is he? You got your spade so dig another grave, man.

(Simon makes one more useless attempt to tidy the graves but he is now even more disturbed by the other man's presence. He looks around apprehensively again before finally going up to Roelf.)

SIMON: When the amagintsa is finished with you they will come and do me. Ja! That is how it is with them. I am too old to run away. They will catch me. "Why you let this whiteman sit here in our world, Simon? Why you let him come and sit here where our people is sleeping." . . . And then they take out their knives again. *(Very firmly)* Is not good! You come with me now.

(Roelf doesn't move. After looking around again Simon prods him with his spade and speaks firmly.)

Hey! I say come with me! Wake up, whiteman. Kom, man!

(Roelf gets slowly to his feet and follows Simon.)

Scene 2

Simon's shack. The two men. Simon lights a candle.

SIMON *(Pointing to a corner)*: You sit there tonight. Tomorrow you go somewhere else.

> *(Roelf sits down in the corner.*
> *Simon goes to what is obviously his bed—a jumble of old blankets on the opposite side—and settles down, resting his back against the wall of the shack.*
> *The candle sits on a wooden box next to Simon's bed. He studies Roelf.)*

ROELF *(Looking around)*: So this is your place . . . your ikhaya . . . your home.

SIMON: Ewe.

ROELF: Ja, well . . . as they say: no place like it, hey? That's for fucking sure.

> *(Shaking his head in disbelief)* If Lorraine—my wife— could see me now! She'd make me soak in Clorox for a

week before she let me get into bed with her. God alone knows what she'd do with you, my friend. Because she's very fussy you know . . . 'specially about bad smells and things like that. Hygiene! That's her hobby. Give her a can of Lysol to spray around . . . you know . . . *(He demonstrates Lorraine spraying the air with aerosol)* Ssssss . . . Sssss . . . and she's a happy woman. Between me and you though I think she carries it a little bit too far. Like this dead woman I'm looking for . . .

SIMON: Red Doek.

ROELF: That's the one. Well, you see, after the accident, I was thinking about her one night . . . well to tell you the truth I was thinking about her every bloody night . . . you know how it is, man, when you switch off the light and you lie there in the dark and your brain just won't stop thinking . . . so I'm lying there in the bed in the dark waiting for the pills to put me to sleep . . . and I was talking to myself, but softly, because I didn't want to wake up Lorraine . . . so I was talking to myself about all that happened and how it happened and about Red Doek, because it just doesn't make sense you see, when the next thing I know is that Lorraine is sitting up in bed and shouting: "Will you please shut up about that bitch! This house already stinks from her! I can smell her everywhere!"

How do you like that hey? She's never seen her but now she can suddenly smell her everywhere. Ja, home sweet home. I know all about it.

SIMON: So why you want to swear at this woman with the red doek? What she do to you?

ROELF: I don't know anymore. I don't know if she did it to me or if I did it to her. All I know is she is dead and I am well and truly fucked-up.

SIMON: What you do to her?

ROELF: That's a nice simple question. I think I killed her!

SIMON: Yo!

ROELF: Yep. Simple as that. Everybody of course says I didn't
. . . the other drivers, the systems manager sitting behind
his desk, my wife . . . Ja! You want to hear Lorraine on that
one! *(Imitating his wife's voice)* "She was drunk, Roofie darling. Booze and pot. It's the same story with all of them."

Thank you very much, Lorrie darling, but I know how
I feel inside. It was me she was looking at when she went
down. It is her face that haunts me every bloody night in
my dreams!

SIMON: How you kill her?

ROELF: Can you read?

*(He takes a very tired newspaper clipping out of a pocket and
offers it to Simon.)*

SIMON *(Shaking his head and waving away the offered clipping)*:
No read.

ROELF: I know . . . it was a stupid bloody question. *(Opens the
clipping and reads)* "December 12, 2000. Mother and child
die on railway tracks." *(Interrupting his reading)* Last
Christmas! You get it? Christmastime? Funny hats and
firecrackers and Father Christmas with a big cotton wool
beard, everybody happy happy happy!

SIMON: Christmas box!

ROELF: Ja, Christmas box. Everybody happy. The big piss-up!
(Resumes reading) "An unidentified woman with a child on
her back stood on the tracks in front of an oncoming train
and she and the baby were pulverized under the train's
wheels. The seriously traumatized train driver looked on
helplessly as . . ." *(Interrupts his reading)* That's me . . . the
"seriously traumatized train driver" is me . . . Roelf Visagie. Do you know what "traumatized" means? Of course
not. It means "fucked-up"! Here . . . *(Tapping his head)* . . .
seriously fucked-up in here, my friend! And did you also

hear "looked on helplessly"? You at least know what that means, don't you? That means that the seriously trauma-tized train driver, who is me, could do fuck-all about it.

That's what they all jump on . . . Lorraine; Dennie, my fishing buddie; Miss Conradie that little poppie with her university diploma hanging on the wall, giving me counsel-ing sessions . . . "You didn't do it, Mr. Visagie. You couldn't stop the train in time. Isn't that so?"

"Yes, Miss Conradie, that is quite right—those big die-sel jobs need fifty meters to stop. She stepped out onto the tracks when there was only about fifteen meters between us."

"There you see. And you couldn't swerve could you?"

"That's also right, Miss Conradie. You can't swerve. But you see, Miss Conradie. I already know all that. So then if it wasn't me, then who was it? God? That's right. Because there was only God and me seeing how it happened. We were the only other ones who saw the look in her eyes, saw the baby's head peeping over her shoulder! So if it wasn't me, then was it *Him*? God Almighty, who was stu-pid enough to make this bloody world in seven days. Yes. Miss Conradie. Stupid. Because I certainly wouldn't. But as it so happens, Miss Conradie, God was only a witness, because it was Roelf Visagie who was tramping down so hard on the brake so that the wheels was screeching on the tracks. It was Roelf Visagie not God there in the cab screaming to her to get out of the fucking way. And it was dear old Roelf again sitting on the side of the tracks vom-iting when he saw how his train had 'pulverized' her and her baby. And finally, Miss Conradie, let me ask you if you think God is also having nightmares every night when he looks into those big eyes with no hope in them."

Yep, Simon. That is what I saw. Eyes that look as hope-less as those graves out there. Eyes that were ready for one of those graves out there.

(Pause. It takes Roelf a good few seconds to recover from his emotional outburst.

Simon waits patiently, staring at him the whole time. Roelf goes back to the clipping and reads again:)

"By Monday night nobody had claimed the bodies from the Mount Road mortuary. In the meantime the train driver is receiving counseling."
There you have it.

(Pause. He carefully folds the clipping and puts it away, shaking his head in disbelief as memories flood back.)

But you know what is interesting, Simon? . . . If you were just watching me from the outside during those first few weeks after it happened you would have said what they all was saying: that Roelf Visagie is getting better. He's getting over it . . . he is on the mend. I tried to keep my mind off things by working in the garden, doing Christmas shopping with Lorraine—that is when we bought the Christmas tree—and just anything else you know that would keep my hands busy. I'm one of those guys that if his hands is busy, he's happy. The one thing that should have warned me that things were cooking up inside me, was the nightmares. Even with the pills that the doctor gave me I would still wake up with the fear of hell in my heart, man, because I was in the cab and she was there on the railway line waiting for me. It was getting so hard on Lorraine, because she had to be at work at the supermarket the next day, that I started sleeping on the pull-out sofa in the lounge. It is easy to see now that that was a big mistake, because that meant I was right in there with the Christmas tree. Breaks my heart, man, when I think about it now. Because we were really all so happy when I put up the tree, and the children decorated it, and I switched on the fairy lights. Lorraine and I had tears in our eyes as we played "Silent Night, Holy Night" on the hi-fi. It didn't happen that night. It was a few nights later. Same old story. I took the sleeping pill, I fell asleep, and then there she was again in front of me, and this time there was also crowds of people on the side of the line watching it happen and cheering like it was some sort of sport going on. I was shit-scared in the dream and I was shit-scared when I was lying there with my eyes wide open because I sort of knew, lying there on the sofa, that she wasn't ever going to go away. So it was once again a case of do something, Roelfie, just get up and do something. There was a second box of fairy lights that I hadn't used, so I decided to put them on the tree as well. I did that and then switched them all on and sat on the sofa looking at them blinking on and off and on and off. If you were sitting there with me now like we are sitting now in this pondok you would have seen me shaking my head because that is what I was doing staring at those lights blinking on and off. It was like a fucking bomb ticking away inside me . . . the lights . . . on and off, on and off . . . and then suddenly "the bomb" is exploding inside me, man. I think I must have looked like a wild animal that escapes from its cage and just wants to kill anything in front of it, anything it sees. And for me it was that stupid bloody Christmas tree blinking on and off and on and off. So I smashed it. Finish and klaar. I ripped the lights out of the wall like they was its roots and I picked up the tree and started smashing it on the floor, and when I was finished there they were standing in the doorway, looking at me with frightened eyes: Lorraine and the kids. She was holding on to them as if I was going to smash them on the floor as well. All I could think of to say was, "What the fucking hell are you all staring at?" And Lorraine said, "These are your children, Roelf Visagie—go swear at your woman from the bush." Then she took the kids into the bedroom and I could hear her lock the door. I heard her say to them, "Jou pa is mal," "Your father's gone mad." But there you have it: "Go swear at your woman from the bush." One day I must tell Lorraine what a big favor she did me when she said that. When I heard those words it was like something just opened up inside me, because I suddenly realized you see that that is what I wanted to do! Ja! I wanted to take a deep breath and then load up my lungs with every dirty thing I had ever heard and then say them into the face of that woman, who still stands there waiting for me in my dreams. I wanted those to be the last words she hears when my train hits her. Can you understand that? Look at what she did to my life, for God's sakes. If she wanted so much to kill herself, why didn't she just take her baby and jump into the river. That would have done it. Why did she have to drag someone else—ME!—into her shit. But the trouble was I didn't know her name!

I mean you know how it is. When you talk to somebody in your mind you think their name, don't you? You don't just say: "Hey you, this" and "Hey you, that." You say their name and then you see them. And that is how the ball started rolling. There in the lounge, with Lorraine and the kids hiding away from me in the bedroom, standing there with the pieces of the Christmas tree lying around me, I suddenly had this wonderful feeling that if I could get her name and swear at her properly, just once, curse and swear her out in English and in Afrikaans, because I really am fully bilingual, everything would once again be all right. I know that sounds stupid now, but I'm telling you the truth, man. I just wanted to swear at her properly. That is how it all started, which ends up with me sitting here with you.

(Pause. A dry little laugh.)

But you see the trouble was nobody could tell me her name! Nobody. Not head office who had the official report of the accident, not the police who spoke to witnesses . . . nobody could tell me who she was! But then it was that Sergeant Boesak there in the Swartkops police station listened to me and seemed to understand what I was going through. He was a good somebody—one of the old-fashioned sort of policemen, you know. It was him who said to me to go the mortuary and see if anybody has identified her dead body because that is where she is lying. Well, to cut a long story short she wasn't there anymore because they had handed the body over to Mr. Mdoda for burial. He had the contract for burying the bodies that nobody wanted. Then Mr. Mdoda sends me to you and now here we sit. Do you understand now, Simon? If I can stand beside her grave it would maybe be even better than just knowing her name. That's why me and you is going to go out there tomorrow and you are going to help me find it. You understand, Simon? One of those graves is hers and we are going to find it tomorrow. And stop shaking your head and looking so scared shitless. I am not going to dig her up for Christ's sake. I just want to curse at her.

(The two men stare at each other. Eventually . . .)

SIMON: I sleep now.

(He blows out the candle.
After a few seconds of silence the scene fades out to the sound of dogs barking and yelping in the background and Simon's snoring.)

SCENE 3

The graveyard.

Simon and Roelf stand in the middle of the graves.

It is another obviously hot day—Roelf is in his shirt sleeves, his jacket is hanging on one of the fence posts. He is making a supreme effort to control his impatience and frustration with Simon.

ROELF: Think, Simon! Maybe four weeks ago Mr. Mdoda comes to you with one big body and one baby body and he say to you put them in the same hole ... *(Holding up his forefinger)* ... Two?

SIMON *(Holding up his forefinger)*: Ewe ... zimbini ... is twee!

ROELF: Yes ... twee! Mr. Mdoda brings them to you ... where did you bury ... where did you dig the hole with your spade?

No! No! Don't shake your head again. Any more head shaking, my friend, and the bloody thing will fall off your shoulders. Just think! Four weeks ... one big body ... one small body ... one hole ... where?

(Simon looks around and then walks among the graves mutter-
ing: "Zimbini, zimbini, zimbini." He is followed by a hopeful
Roelf who in turn is muttering: "One big one, one small one,
one hole." Simon eventually pauses and looks down at a grave.
An excited and suddenly apprehensive Roelf backs away.)

This one?

SIMON: I think . . . *(For a moment it looks as if he might be on the*
point of saying yes but in the end he shakes his head) . . . No . . .
not this one.

ROELF *(Increasingly desperate)*: No! Don't stop. Look some
more. What about these over here?

(Simon follows Roelf.)

This one hey? Or this one? Look at this one, Simon. It
looks like it's quite a new one.

SIMON *(Finally nodding his head)*: Ewe . . . ewe . . . is just so.

ROELF *(Staring down at the grave in disbelief)*: Jesus! This is
hers? This is where you . . . dis twee?

SIMON: Ewe, ja, dis twee . . . this is where the dogs come last
week and try to dig. So I must fill it up again. Two times!
But it's an old, old one not a new one. But the dogs dig
deep and so when I fill it up it is looking like new one.

(Roelf is now very angry and on the point of violence. A fright-
ened Simon backs away from him. It is a dangerous moment.)

ROELF: What the fuck is going on with you, old man? Are you
playing around with me? Do you think this is some sort of
fucking game? Because if that's what you think it is, then
you are playing with fire, old man. If you don't find her
grave for me without any more farting around I'll take
your bloody spade and dig up every one of them until I do
find her . . . and then I'll dig a nice deep hole for you and
I bloody well mean it!

(Leaving Simon and wandering among the graves) Christ Almighty, just look at them. Look! Open your bloody eyes, old man, and look at them. This place is a bloody disgrace to humanity!

(He stops at one of the graves, which has got a rusty motorcar muffler on it.)

Have you got no respect for the dead? Because if that is the case then you are worse than those dogs in the bush. And you know why? Because these are human beings lying here and you are also supposed to be one as well.

(He picks up the muffler and throws it away. In its place he picks up one of the stones on the grave.)

If you got to mark them, use these, for God's sake. They're not flowers but God did at least make them as well. And what's more . . . Ja! . . . *(An excited little laugh as an idea occurs to him)* . . . Ja! . . . you can even make a cross with them! Yes! Look . . . *(On his hands and knees, placing stones on the graves)* See how easy it is. Long one down for his legs and then a short one across for his arms. Come on, Simon. Look! Doesn't that look better.

(Simon is watching Roelf's deranged behavior with disbelief and fear.
Roelf moves to another grave where he makes another cross. His behavior is becoming increasingly absurd.)

Don't just stand there . . . roll up your sleeves and help me. You fetch more stones and I'll make the cross . . . I know how to do it, you see. You might make the cross upside down and I think that's the way they do it in devil worship. You'd be sending the poor bugger in the grave to Hell instead of Heaven. Ja. That's the way it works you see. You should see my mother's grave. Lorraine and I took the children there a few days before Christmas to pray for her and wish her a happy Christmas in Heaven. And flowers. A big bunch of . . . beautiful flowers . . .

(Simon approaches Roelf warily.)

SIMON: Stop now, whiteman . . .

(Roelf has moved to another grave.)

Whiteman! . . . Stop now . . .
ROELF: Stop what?
SIMON: Stop what you doing.
ROELF: What I'm doing is respecting the dead. You are the one who must stop putting junk on their graves.
SIMON *(Now beginning to sense Roelf's inner distress. He speaks firmly but gently)*: You must stop now looking for her.
ROELF: For who?
SIMON: For Red Doek.
ROELF: Red Doek? . . .

(For a few seconds the name means nothing to him. When he realizes who Simon is talking about, his hands, filled with stones, fall limply to his side.)

That's right . . . Red Doek . . . I'm looking for her . . . *(Speaking very quietly)* . . . and her baby . . . You realize, don't you, Simon, that it was a woman . . . a mother . . . with her baby on her back that stepped out on to the rails . . . there in front of me . . . and waited . . . for me . . . for the end . . . staring . . . and waiting . . .

(Pause. He looks at the stones in his hands and slowly makes one more cross on the grave in front of him. He then crawls away and sits again with his back up against a fence post.)

(Speaking quietly) My head is all fucked-up isn't it. Totally deurmekaar now. My ma was like that before she died. Didn't even recognize me anymore. Called me "Ferdie." Where the hell did that come from? There's no fucking Ferdie in our family.

(Pause.)

You see, Simon . . . the trouble is I keep seeing Red Doek's big brown eyes . . . flat nose . . . just like yours . . . her mouth closed tight . . . I keep seeing that in my head all the time like it was . . . you know . . . when she stood there.

(Pause.)

But she doesn't look like that now, does she? I mean . . . things happen to you down there in the ground . . . not so? It's not like the deep freeze we got at home—put in the nice fish you caught in the river and take it out six weeks later and there it is . . . good as new . . . thaw it out, salt and pepper and a big piece of butter in the frying pan . . . and there you have it. Fresh fried fish. But down there . . . things happen, hey? Worms and all that. Like what happened to poor old Arnie Vosloo in the *Mummy* pictures where he is the king of Egypt and climbs out of his grave—bits of flesh hanging on the bones, worms crawling around in his eyeball. Jesus! Makes you think, doesn't it? All of them . . . some mother's children . . . one day you and me also . . . *(Gestures to the graves)* . . . and that's how it ends for everybody. Yes . . . make no mistake, my friend . . . black man or white man . . . the worms don't care about that . . . it's all the same to them . . .

(Another twilight is settling in. A few yelps and howls from dogs in the bush. Both men look in their direction.)

SIMON: I think the dogs come tonight.

ROELF: And they don't give a shit either, do they, about white or black . . . and you know what we call them, white men—the dogs? Man's best friend! How's that for a joke! (*Mirthless little laugh*) That's a good one hey? We got one of those little ones with curly white hair. Lorraine calls it Baby. I don't like it. Growls at me all the time. Bloody sure he'd like to dig me up one day when I'm dead.

SIMON: When I was little inkwenkwana I had two dogs. One white one and one black one.

ROELF: Like me and you, hey? One white and one black! What was their names?

SIMON: The white one I call him iWandle because he is white like the sea when it washes the rocks. The black one is Indudumo . . .

ROELF: Indudumo . . .

SIMON: Ja, the big noise in the sky when the rain is coming.

ROELF: Thunder.

SIMON: Ja! Thunder in the sky.

ROELF: So where were you when you were a little boy . . . where was your home?

SIMON: My home was far away, by Hluleka and my name that time was Andile. Andile Hanabe. Simon is my whiteman's name.

ROELF: And you were happy.

SIMON: Ewe . . . because I walk all the time with my dogs by the sea and I try to catch the fish.

ROELF: With a fishing rod?

SIMON (*Shaking his head vigorously*): Aikona! Is iWandle and Indudumo who do it.

ROELF: They catch the fish?

SIMON: Ja. They good dogs. They see him the fish. There in the big gat with the water in it.

ROELF: The rock pool.

SIMON: They see the fish in the water. They see him and they start barking and barking and I look and I also see him. So then I jump in the water they also jump in. We chase the fish in that gat, man. He go this way and that way but we chase him, and then is iWandle who bite him and he jump and I catch him. Ja! I catch him when he jump.

ROELF: With your hands?

SIMON: Ja! With my hands I catch him.

ROELF: A big one?

SIMON: Yo! Is a big one. That one time is a big one and I make my mother and my little sister very happy. *(Smiling as he smacks his lips)* Ja. We like fry fish.

ROELF: Yes . . . 'specially with nice soft fried potatoes.

(Neither of them moves as the twilight deepens into night.)

SIMON: Come on, Roofie . . . is getting dark and dangerous. We must go sit inside now. Come.

Scene 4

Simon's shack.

Simon ladles out baked beans from a tin onto an old enamel plate. That done, he breaks half a loaf of white bread into two pieces. He takes one of the pieces, the tin with what's left of the beans, and a spoon to Roelf, who is sitting quietly in his corner.

Simon then settles down with the plate and eats with relish.

SIMON: Roelfie, here's your beans.

It is like I tell you—the amagintsa is there by the shop and they stop me and speak: "Where you get the money, old man?" I don't tell them you give it. I tell them I save it. But I see they don't believe me. So they grab me and say to me: "Be careful, old man. We come to visit you one night." So there it is. I think they hear about you, Roofie.

ROELF: Let them come. I'm not scared of a bunch of tsotsis.

SIMON: Hey, Roofie! You don't know this world.

ROELF: What don't I know about your world, Andile?

SIMON: Amagintsa is like the dogs in the bush, always smelling for new ones to dig up and eat. Just so with the amagintsa. They are smelling you out now, Roofie. Very soon they will find you and eat you with their knives. Dogs got long teeth, amagintsa got sharp knives. Pasop, witman!

(Simon eats. Roelf watches him, but his beans and bread remain untouched.)

ROELF: Simon, do you believe in ghosts? You know, spoke. Are there spoke out there? . . . You know . . . from the dead people.
SIMON: *Spirits! Spoke!*
ROELF: That's right . . . spoke. Are their spoke out there?
SIMON: Ewe. Plenty of spoke out there.
ROELF: Do you see them, Simon?
SIMON: I hear them. At night. When the dogs are digging I hear them. They don't like the dogs. So I go out and throw stones. I throw very good because I always hear one of them cry in the dog language: "Yeeeee!" *(Laughs)* And then I hear the ghosts again. It is like the wind, Roefie. It is very sad. The dogs wake them up and they are not happy.
ROELF: Do you speak to them?
SIMON: I sing to them. I sing like my mother sing to me when I was a little boy and she carry me on her back.

(Simon sings a Zula lullaby in Xhosa: "Thula, Mama, Thula!":)

Imfene mam' imfene yamthabath' umntwana.
Wasuke wakhala wathi, "Iyo." (x2)

Khawuthule, Mama, thula, thula, Mama, thula.
Thula, Mama, Thula, thula yithi tu! (x2)

Yamthabath' umntwana yambeka egxeni.
Wasuk wakhala wathi, "Iyo." (x2)

(Translation: "Hush, Mother, Don't Cry!"

The baboon took the baby.
The baby cried out, "Iyo."

Hush, Mother, don't cry.
Hush, Mother, hush!

The baboon put the baby over his shoulder.
The baby cried out, "Iyo.")

ROELF: You think they hear you?
SIMON: Ewe. They go back to sleep . . . And all is quiet again.

(Pause.)

ROELF: Tell me, Simon, when you bury one of them are you by
    yourself? When is it just you there by the . . . what do you
    call it . . . the hole where you put them in . . . the grave?
SIMON: The incgwaba. Sometimes Mr. Mdoda stay and watch
    me dig.
ROELF: So what do you feel, Simon. You know . . . when you
    put them in the grave . . . what do you feel in your heart
    . . . inside you.
SIMON: I am happy. Because Mr. Mdoda pay me.
ROELF: I know that, but don't you feel a bit sorry for them? A
    little bit sad?
SIMON: No.
ROELF: Then why do you put something on the grave . . . every
    grave you put something on it.
SIMON: Because I mustn't dig there again. When Mr. Mdoda
    first give me the job I sometimes dig and then I see some-

body is already sleeping there. So now I put something on
top to tell me: "No, Simon, someone is already sleeping
here." Why you ask me so much?

ROELF: Why? . . . Because . . . because it's one of your own
people, for God's sake. It was certainly somebody's . . .
I don't know . . . husband or brother, if it was a man; or
somebody's mother or sister or wife, if it was a woman.
One thing I know for sure is that, if I had to dig a hole
and put one of my people in it, I'd have some very strange
feelings inside me . . . even if I didn't know their name or
who they were or what they were.

*(Pause. He is moving into unknown territory and is not sure of
where he will end up.)*

But you know what's even more strange, Simon? . . .

SIMON: Wat is even more strange?

ROELF *(Not easy for him)*: Out there this afternoon . . . there in
the graves . . . when I got so difficult with you because you
couldn't show me where Red Doek was buried . . . I got so
cross with you because I was . . . Because . . . Ja! Because
I was having strange feelings for all those poor buggers
lying there and turning into mummies. Can you believe
that? *(A little snort of disbelief)* Ja! And because it was like
that . . . the next thing I know is—you are not going to
believe this but I swear to God it's true—the next thing
I know is that I didn't want to swear at her anymore! Can
you also believe that? It's true, man! I didn't want to swear
at her because . . . I was thinking . . . I was thinking about
those pondoks in the bush, about the smell of shit, about the
man who asked me if I wanted to fuck a black woman . . .
and I was thinking . . . she lived in one of those pondoks
. . . she lived like that . . . Ja! That was what Red Doek
called home. A young woman, a mother, with her baby!
You get it? That is fucking hopeless, man. Think about

it. Wouldn't you also want to go stand on a railway line and wait for the next train if that is all life has to offer you and your baby? And then to make it worse . . . she ends up here . . . in one of your ingiwabas or whatever you call them. And why? . . . Because that is still not the end . . . Because the big happy ending is that Nobody Wants Her! . . . Except the dogs.

(He takes the press clipping out of his pocket) Remember what it said? Nobody came to claim her! Nobody wants her! And when we start looking . . . even we can't find her.

(He takes a few seconds to regain control of his emotions.)

(Speaking very simply) But suppose we did, Simon. Suppose you remembered where you buried a woman with a little baby, and you take me to that grave. What do I do? You understand now? I don't want to swear at her anymore. What do I do? Go buy flowers to put there in place of the rubbish you put on it? That will help her a hell of a lot, won't it. Or say a prayer? To Him? *(Pointing up)* If I ever get around to talking to Him it won't be an "Asseblief Heilige Genadige God" / "Please Most Holy and Merciful God" prayer that comes out of my mouth. You can rest assured of that, my friend.

SIMON: And now you want to see her ghost?

ROELF: I know. Maybe.

SIMON: And you want to speak to her ghost? Yo!

ROELF: Why not, for God's sake . . . If you can sing to them, why can't I speak if there is things I want to say to her . . . or ask her . . . Oh fuck it . . . I don't know. And neither do you, my friend. *(Defensively)* So stop looking at me like you now also think I am crazy.

SIMON *(Shaking his head)*: Eat your boontjies, Roofie.

ROELF *(Pushing his food in Simon's direction)*: I'm not hungry. You can have them.

(Simon takes the tin and wastes no time in tucking into it.
Roelf sits back and stares into space.
The scene fades out on the image of the two men.)

SCENE 5

Night.

In the dimly lit interior of the shack we see Roelf stand up and quietly leave to walk among the graves.

ROELF: Red Doek? I don't know your name, so that is what Simon and I call you. He is the man who buried you.

(Pause.)

Can you hear me? I want to talk to you . . . but . . . it's sort of stupid . . . I don't really know where you are. Are you lying here in the ground. Or are you up in Heaven? Not Hell—no ways. That's for sure. If all they say about God Almighty is true—that he loves all of us—then you are certainly not down there at the big barbeque. Miss Conradie told me not to worry so much because "your soul is now at rest." Like hell, hey! At rest? When your last memory of life is a white man staring at you from the cab of a diesel locomotive as you go down under its wheels? So what I am going to do, Red Doek, is imagine Simon is right, and that your ghost comes out of the grave at night and walks around here at night . . . that I can talk to you like you was standing right here in front of me . . . listening to me.

(Pause.)

It's strange, you know. Sometimes I think I've got so much to say to you that this one night won't be long enough . . . but then at other times I think there is nothing to say . . . that for me you will forever just be Red Doek standing there on the tracks, and that for you I will forever just be a white man staring at you in the few seconds before you die. But that is not right, is it? It can't be as simple as that! I mean . . . look what has happened . . . to us . . . to me and you. You and your baby are dead . . . buried in one of these ingiwabas and I am . . . I don't know what. I'm trying all the time to understand it all, but all I know is that you are dead, and Roelf Visagie is fucked-up in his head like never before. So what it comes down to is that it is all about you and me and that is what makes it so complicated for me. You see, I don't really know what your story is—who you are, where you come from, what's your name . . . that sort of thing. It's not so bad now as it was at the beginning when all I could say to myself was that my train . . . Me! . . . Roelf Visagie . . . killed a black woman with a red doek and a baby on her back. But now, thanks to all I've seen and heard in the past few weeks, like that walk in the Swartkops bush looking for your pondok, thanks to all I've thought and what Simon has said to me and what this place looks like, I got some sort of idea, some sort of feeling about your world. You see, Red Doek, most of us white people got no idea about what it's

like because our world is so different! We always think
we know—like Lorraine, my wife—she thinks she knows
everything about you people . . . and I did as well . . . but
the truth is we don't.

But now, like I said, I got some ideas . . . I got some
good guesses going about your world and why you stood
there on the railway line, waiting for me and my train.
One of my guesses is that I think it's all about hope. You
know what I mean—hope!—hoping good things are
going to happen to you, that tomorrow is going to be better than today, which was terrible. And there you have it.

(Pause.)

I don't know what it is like to live without hope, to give up.

Because you did, didn't you? That is why you did what
you did because you didn't believe anymore that good
things was going to happen to you and your baby. I'm
thinking about it all the time now, trying to imagine what
it was like for you. It is very dark in Simon's shack when
he blows out the candle, so I lie there in that dark and
I think to myself . . . was it like this for her? Was it dark
like this for Red Doek? Darker . . . I say . . . because her
darkness was somehow inside her and how the hell do you
light a stompie candle there? When I think about that,
when I try to imagine what that is like, I get frightened.
Yes! Believe it or not, but I still get scared of the dark.

So then . . . what now you ask? I've got to do something! I know it's too late for you to do anything, but I still
got a chance. What's more, Red Doek, it feels very urgent
that I do something, because it feels like I am losing you,
and if that happens, if I can't even remember your face
anymore, then I really will go mad like they all say I am.
But I am not, and to prove it I know what I must do now.
I've got a newspaper story here in my pocket which is all

about me and you . . . there is one thing that always sort of upsets me in a special way when I read it . . . it's where it says that "nobody claimed her." Did you know that? Did you know that when you and your baby was lying there in the Mount Road mortuary, nobody came to claim you? A mother and her baby and nobody wanted them! Can you believe that? Because you know what the Bible says, don't you? We was all made in His image . . . you . . . me . . . Simon . . . every human being . . . made in His image. But now you are lying here in the place for the ones without names because nobody wanted you. Well that is not the way it is anymore, because now I hold up my hand and say: "I Claim Her!" Me . . . Roelf Visage . . . the driver of the train what killed her . . . wants her to be his. Finish and klaar. You are mine . . . and God is my witness tonight even as he was when it all happened. You see, Red Doek, if I did lose you . . . if I ever, for one day, forget what happened to me and you there between Perseverance and Dispatch, then God must send me off to Hell when I die.

(Simon comes out of the darkness.)

Scene 6

The shack. Evening. The candle is lit.

Another meal. This time Simon is spooning out smooth apricot jam onto half a loaf of white bread, which he hands over to Roelf. He then settles down to eat the other half.

Roelf is quieter and seemingly at peace with himself.

SIMON: Roofie! There is bread and apricot jam. Come, Roofie, let's eat. You like, Roofie? Apricot jam.

ROELF: Ja. I like.

SIMON: Ja . . . is lekker! A little sweetness is good.

ROELF: The best is golden syrup on fresh white bread when it is still nice and warm. You ever had that?

SIMON: Never.

ROELF: You must try it some time. Lyle's Golden Syrup. When I was a little boy and we didn't have jam or syrup my ma use to sprinkle white sugar on my bread.

SIMON: When I was young there by Hluleka, me and my father, used to look for wild honey in the bush. It's also nice.

(Pause. Roelf still hasn't touched his bread and jam.)

So what you thinking, Roofie?

ROELF: Nothing.

SIMON: Then why you no eat? Why you say nothing?

ROELF: Nothing more to say, Simon. So I was just thinking about going home. I can't stay here.

SIMON: Is good you go home. When you go?

ROELF: I don't know.

SIMON: Maybe tomorrow is good.

ROELF: Maybe.

SIMON: Why you not say yes, Roofie?

ROELF: Because . . . I don't know . . . Because . . . Ja! . . . Because it doesn't feel like it is finished yet.

SIMON: What?

ROELF: Simon . . . What *this*? Why *that*? I don't know every bloody thing!

(Pause.)

Being here doesn't feel finished.

(Simon stares at him uncomprehendingly.)

You understand, don't you?

SIMON *(Shaking his head)*: No.

ROELF: Well, don't let it give you sleepless nights, my friend, because to tell you the truth . . . neither do I. I want to go home to Lorraine, my kids, Prissie and Morné, even the fucking dog Baby. But something is holding me back. We are never going to find her grave out there. I don't want to swear at her anymore. Just the opposite, man. She's mine now. Simon, she is now mine . . . you understand? I don't want to swear at her anymore because now she's mine. I claimed her.

SIMON *(Shocked)*: What you saying? You want to marry her?

ROELF: Oh for God's sake, Simon, give me a break!

SIMON: She's lying in the ground and you want to marry her?

ROELF: No, man, you didn't understand me. It's not like that!
It's more like . . . let's just say I don't know what it means
when I say she is mine, but I know she is because I feel
that way inside my heart and so I claimed her. Nobody
else wanted her Simon . . . I do, and that's the end of it.

And I will also tell you that I know when that happened
. . . when she became mine like nothing else in my life has
ever really been mine before . . . it was when we looked
into each other's eyes in the few seconds before she and
her baby died . . . underneath me. And you want to know
something else, Simon? Maybe it was like that for her
also. Ja! Have you thought about that? That I was the last
human being she saw. There was no hatred in her eyes,
you know, Simon, no anger . . . just me . . . she saw me.

(Pause.)

If I had known then what I know now, if I had felt then
what I feel now, then I would have asked them there in the
mortuary to let me bury her. I mean it.

(Pause.)

But I didn't . . . and maybe that is what it's all about . . .
maybe that's why this doesn't feel like it is finished.

(Pause. Simon is staring silently at Roelf.)

Come on, man. You of all people must know what I mean.
You take your spade and then you dig a hole . . . you dig
it nice and deep so that the dogs can't get at it . . . you put
the body in . . . right? . . . And then you put all the sand

43

back on top of it . . . not so? No . . . I almost forgot . . . you put something on top of it so that you don't dig there again. But then it's over. Finished. You walk away. That's what I can't do, Simon. Walk away.

(Simon, eating bread and jam, is studying Roelf thoughtfully. After a few seconds, he pushes his food aside, stands up slowly, goes to the doorway and looks out over the graves.)

SIMON: Roofie . . .

ROELF: Ja?

SIMON: How many is sleeping there?

ROELF: I don't know. If you want me to, I'll count them all for you tomorrow.

SIMON: Tomorrow there is one more. Mr. Mdoda see me there at the shop when I am buy the jam and he tell me he bring me another nameless one tomorrow.

ROELF: Okay. I'll count them after you've buried him.

SIMON *(Shaking his head, he turns and faces Roelf)*: No. Not me.

(He fetches his spade and offers it to Roelf.)

You must dig the hole.

ROELF: Me? Why me?

SIMON: Because you must put her in.

ROELF: It's a woman?

SIMON: I don't know. But we say it is a woman. We say it is Red Doek. So tomorrow you bury Red Doek.

ROELF: What the hell is going on with you, Simon.

SIMON: Is just like you said, Roelfie. You dig . . . you dig deep hole . . . then you put her in . . . then you cover her up. Then you go get stones and put them like you like it on top . . . and then, Roelfie . . . I think then it is finished for you . . . and you can walk away . . . you can go home.

(Roelf takes the spade.)

ROELF: Okay.

(Simon goes to his corner, settles down, then blows out the candle. After a few seconds of darkness . . .)

Simon!

(A few more seconds of silence and then we hear Simon's snoring.)

I'll do it . . .

(There is enough dim light in the shack for us to see Roelf stand up and quietly leave. Still holding the spade, he stands among the graves for a few seconds, then goes to the spot that Simon marked as the next grave. He starts digging.
Lights fade out completely on Roelf digging.)

Epilogue

SIMON: This is where we find him. Here in the ground. In this hole is where the amagintsa bury him after they kill him. Roofie himself was digging this hole when the amagintsa come. Ewe! One time in the night I wake up and I see Roofie is gone, so I look outside and I see him here digging. I call him, but he says he is digging the hole for the new one that Mr. Mdoda is bringing, and that I must go back and sleep. So I go back and sleep, but then I wake up again and I hear the amagintsa come. I hear the shouting and swearing . . . and then it is all quiet. When Mr. Mdoda come in the morning with the new nameless one for me to bury, we come here and we see there is blood, a lot of blood all around here. So Mr. Mdoda ask me what happens here, so I tell him about Roofie. Mr. Mdoda gets very cross and swears at me, and then he goes and fetches the polisie. When they come, they make me dig here, and then we find Roofie. Kaalgat. No clothes. That's how the amagintsa leave him. The polisie grab me and say:

"Why you kill the whiteman with your spade?" But I say to them: "No! It wasn't me!" So the policeman says that I lie and that I am drunk because "there is blood on the spade." But I say to them: "No . . . I am not drunk. It is the amagintsa who kill him. They take out their knives and do it." And then Mr. Mdoda who is also standing there tells them: "Yes, it is the amagintsa who did it." So then the policeman say to me: "Why you let this whiteman die here? Why you let him mess with our people?" So then I do what Mr. Mdoda tell me to do: I tell them I don't know the whiteman. I never seen him before. Then they take him away and also my spade. And I say: "No, you mustn't take my spade, because I must bury the new one." Then the black policeman tells me they must take the spade because there is blood on it. When they are gone Mr. Mdoda tells me he is finished with me and that he will get somebody else to bury the new nameless one. So there it is. I haven't got a job and now also I haven't got a spade.

(He stands there, his hands held out in a helpless gesture.)

END OF PLAY

Coming Home

For Marianne McDonald

Production History

Coming Home received its world premiere at the Long Wharf Theatre (Gordon Edelstein, Artistic Director; Joan Channick, Managing Director) in New Haven, Connecticut, on January 21, 2009. The production was directed by Gordon Edelstein; the set designer was Eugene Lee, the costume designer was Jessica Ford, the lighting designer was Stephen Strawbridge, the sound designer was Corrine Livingston, the stage manager was Jason Kaiser. The cast was:

VERONICA JONKERS	Roslyn Ruff
MANNETJIE JONKERS	Namumba Santos (younger); Mel Eichler (older)
ALFRED WITBOOI	Colman Domingo
OUPA JONKERS	Lou Ferguson

The play received its west coast premiere at The Fountain Theatre (Deborah Lawlor, Producing Artistic Director; Stephen Sachs, Co-Artistic Director; Simon Levy, Producing Director/Dramaturg) in Los Angeles, on June 20, 2009. The production was directed by Stephen Sachs; the set designer was Laura Fine Hawkes, the costume designer was Shon Le Blanc, the lighting designer was Christian Epps, the sound designer/composer was Peter Bayne, the production stage manager was Liz McGavock. The cast was:

VERONICA JONKERS	Deidrie Henry
MANNETJIE JONKERS	Timothy Taylor (younger);
	Matthew Elam,
	Noah Murtadha (older)
ALFRED WITBOOI	Thomas Silcott
OUPA JONKERS	Adolphus Ward

The play opened at The Wilma Theater (Blanka Zizka and Jiri Zizka, Co-Artistic Directors; James Haskins, Managing Director) in Philadelphia, on October 21, 2009. The production was directed by Blanka Zizka; the set and costume designer was Anne Patterson, the lighting designer was Thom Weaver, the sound designer was Andrea Sotzing, the dramaturg was Walter Bilderback, the stage manager was Patreshettarlini Adams. The cast was:

VERONICA JONKERS	Patrice Johnson
MANNETJIE JONKERS	Elijah Felder (younger);
	Antonio J. Dandridge (older)
ALFRED WITBOOI	Nyambi Nyambi
OUPA JONKERS	Lou Ferguson

The play opened at Berkeley Repertory Theatre (Tony Taccone, Artistic Director; Susan Medak, Managing Director) in Berkeley, on January 20, 2010. The production was directed by Gordon Edelstein; the set designer was Eugene Lee, the costume designer was Jessica Ford, the lighting/projection designer was Stephen Strawbridge, the sound designer was Corrine K. Livingston, the stage manager was Michael Suenkel. The cast was:

VERONICA JONKERS	Roslyn Ruff
MANNETJIE JONKERS	Kohle T. Bolton (younger);
	Jaden Malik Wiggins (older)
ALFRED WITBOOI	Thomas Silcott
OUPA JONKERS	Lou Ferguson

Characters

VERONICA JONKERS: a young woman in her late twenties.

MANNETJIE JONKERS: Veronica's son; about five years old when we first see him.

ALFRED WITBOOI: the same age as Veronica.

OUPA JONKERS: Veronica's grandfather, an old man.

Time

The action of the play takes place over a period of about five years, starting in 2002.

And the end of all our exploring
Will be to arrive where we started
And know the place for the first time.

—*T. S. Eliot*
"Little Gidding,"
Four Quartets

Morning star lights the way;
Restless dream all done;
Shadows gone, break of day,
Life has just begun.
Every tear wiped away,
Pain and sickness gone;
Wide awake there with Him!
Peace goes on and on!
Going home, going home,
I'll be going home.
See the light! See the sun!
I'm just going home.

—*Gospel hymn*

Act One

―――――

SCENE I

A bleak little room. Late afternoon sunlight is pouring in through the room's one window. There is a door at the far wall, a simple table with two chairs in the center of the room, and a bed with a mattress (no linen) against the wall on one side. On the opposite side of the room is a sagging line with an old blanket draped over it, obviously meant to curtain off and make private a corner space.

The door opens. Veronica and Mannetjie enter hesitantly. They are loaded up with a variety of bundles and an old and battered suitcase. They remain standing on the threshold for a few seconds, looking at the room.

VERONICA: This is it. Oupa's house.

> *(She enters the room and wanders around, ending up at the bed, where she sits. She registers Mannetjie, still standing uncertainly at the door.)*

Sorry, my darling. Put your parcels down and come sit here with Mommy.

(Mannetjie joins her on the bed. Veronica puts an arm around him.)

It's just so strange being back here. So many memories. This was Mommy's home when she was a little girl. Me and Oupa. In here.

All those stories Mommy was telling you about me as a little girl . . . in here. Grandma Betty died when I was still very small, so after that it was just me and Oupa in here. That hokkie there behind the curtain, that was my place. Oupa slept on this bed. Ja. Supper and breakfast time at that table. I did all the cooking, even when I was still only a small little girl. 'Specially Oupa's favorite . . . Boontjie soup with some pieces of nice fat mutton. So what do you think? Like it?

MANNETJIE *(Shaking his head disconsolately)*: No. I don't like it.

VERONICA: I know, my darling. Mommy knows it doesn't look nice now, but you just wait and see. Mommy is going to fix it up and then it will look very different.

(She leaves the bed and goes to the other side of the room with the makeshift curtain. She takes it down, bundles it up and throws it into a corner.)

Good-bye to that piece of rubbish. We'll find something special to hang here because this is now going to be the room of Mr. Manfred Jonkers. And who is he?

MANNETJIE: Me.

VERONICA: That's right. This is going to be your very own room just as it was mine. We'll get pictures of animals and paste them all over the wall. You would like that, wouldn't you?

MANNETJIE: Yes, Mommy.

VERONICA: We'll cut them out of magazines. That's what I did in here when I was a little girl. But no animals for little Veronica. She wanted pictures of Eartha Kitt. Lena Horne and of course Mama Africa . . . Miriam Makeba. Those were my pinups. But that's not all we're going to do in here. You just wait and see. Mommy's got ideas, Mannetjie.

(Another tour of the room.)

Pretty curtain on this window, nice tablecloth, some other pictures on the wall. We'll make the bed a sort of sofa with a lot of cushions the way they do it in Cape Town . . . A doormat so that we must all wipe our feet clean when we come in here . . .

(She has reached a little shelf next to the door—it holds a collection of small tins. A little laugh as she takes one of them and shakes it. Something rattles inside.)

He kept all his seeds in these.

(She opens it and goes back to Mannetjie on the bed.)

Hold out your hand.

(She empties the contents into his hand.)

Do you know what these are?

MANNETJIE: No.

VERONICA: Pumpkin seeds! If you plant these in the ground they will grow and then one day you will get big white pumpkins. But do you know what Oupa called these? "Little Miracles"! Yes. That is what he said. Every one of these seeds was a little miracle. *(Imitating her oupa's voice)*

"Miracles, Veronica. All my seeds are miracles. And you know why? When you plant them, they will one day turn into big, flat, white Boer Pampoens."

I thought Oupa was just being silly, you know—calling them miracles!—because that is something only Jesus can do. But not anymore. You know why? Because now I also got my own miracle. You! Once upon a time you were also just a small little seed inside Mommy and now look . . . you have turned into a big boy . . . who will one day turn into a big man.

Poor old wonderful Oupa. If only he could have lived long enough to see you, Mannetjie. And for you to see him! Mommy still can. Ja. The way he would walk in through the door, and hang his old tin mug on that nail sticking out of the shelf. Still there. Can you see it?

(She is on her legs again, moving in sync with her memories of the old man.)

After that, straight to the table. I tell Oupa he must try to imagine he is sitting in the big steak house in Graaff-Reinet. I fold the dishcloth nicely and hang it on my arm and then I make a big fuss about wiping the table:

"Good evening, Mr. Jonkers. Tonight we got steak, chops, boerewors, and pickled fish on the menu, and our special is sardines chili-chili."

I change the menu every time but then Oupa makes me cross because he always orders bean soup with pieces of fat mutton. I try to trick him sometimes and say there's no bean soup on the menu tonight and he must choose something else.

But he doesn't change his mind—he just wants his bean soup! So then I serve him the same old boontjie soup with fat mutton because that is what I mostly cook for him. The one thing Oupa could never understand is about tips.

I always had to tell him that ten cents was not a proper tip for a big meal. Believe me, Mannetjie, the two of us was happy in here. And so will we be. We'll make our own games in here. It's not a very fancy little room, I know . . . but better than that pondok we were living in on the Cape Flats, hey, Mannetjie?

(Shaking her head at the memory) No wragty . . . never again! That's a promise, my darling. Mommy will rather scrub floors in all the white people's houses in this village than go back there again.

MANNETJIE: Mommy?

VERONICA: Yes, my darling?

MANNETJIE: I'm thirsty.

VERONICA: Sorry, my darling! Mommy is just so excited and mixed-up about being back.

(She opens a plastic supermarket bag and takes out a large Pepsi bottle—it is half full of water. She unscrews the cap and hands the bottle over to Mannetjie. He is on the point of drinking from the bottle when she stops him.)

No wait . . . wait . . . give me back the bottle.

(She fetches Oupa's old tin mug, still hanging from the nail above the shelf and, after wiping it out, pours water into it. She hands it to Mannetjie and watches him drink.)

You must drink out of Oupa's mug. He took it with him to the akkers every day. When it was school holidays I would take him his sandwiches at lunchtime. He was always sitting there under a big walnut tree waiting for me and drinking water out of this mug. It was pumped up by the windmill from deep in the ground. Ice cold water, Mannetjie . . . like there was a fridge down there. He used to say to me that once you've had a drink of Karoo water, you will always come back. He was right. Here I am! And there you are also. Yes! You've now also drunk Karoo water. So now we are going to make a toast. I lift up the bottle and you lift up your mug and we say, "To Oupa." You ready? Come now, Mannetjie . . . please, say it with Mommy.

(He lifts up his mug and together with his mother says, "To Oupa." Veronica wipes away a tear.)

"Snot en trane." That's what he always said when I cried. "Snot en trane, my kind."

MANNETJIE: Is there any Marie biscuits left, Mommy?

VERONICA *(Mock surprise)*: What? So now you also want to have a party?

(A half-eaten packet of biscuits comes out of the bag.)

Of course you can have some biscuits. But we must also keep some for breakfast tomorrow. Then we will go to the shop and buy bread and things. This is home now, Mannetjie . . . we've come home . . . and we are going to have lots and lots of real parties in here . . . birthday parties, Christmas parties . . . just you wait and see. Now take off your shoes and lie down and have a nice long sleep. We'll unpack the suitcase tomorrow.

(Mannetjie begins taking off his shoes and Veronica retrieves a blanket from their pile of parcels. There is a knock on the door. A sudden spasm of city-bred fear in mother and child. Veronica stops what she is doing and goes to her son's side. She signs to him to be silent. The knocking comes again.)

MAN'S VOICE: I know you're in there.

(Pause.)

Open up!

(Pause.)

Veronica!

VERONICA: Who are you?

MAN'S VOICE: What's the matter with you? Don't you remember? It's me.

VERONICA: Who's me?

MAN'S VOICE: Alfred! Open the door.

VERONICA: Alfred Witbooi?

MAN'S VOICE: Of course. Now hurry up. Open the door.

(Veronica, laughing, hurries to the door and opens it. Alfred Witbooi enters. He is burdened with a huge collection of kitchen utensils, pots and pans, an old zinc bath and a bucket, all piled up precariously in his arms.)

ALFRED: Come help me with these things. It feels like my arms is going to fall off. I want to see if you are still so pretty as you were.

VERONICA: And I want to see if you are still just so ugly.

(Both of them find this inordinately funny. The joy of seeing each other again erupts in a gale of laughter as Veronica helps him unload his things. When it is done, their laughter subsides and they stand staring at each other.)

My God! Alfred Witbooi. Yes, it's you all right . . . only uglier.

ALFRED: It's almost like old times, hey. Me and you.

VERONICA: So what you doing knocking on doors in the middle of the night. You should be in bed having your beauty sleep.

ALFRED: And you also, Veronica Jonkers.

63

(Another gale of laughter. Mannetjie sits silently on his bed watching them.)

VERONICA *(Referring to the pile of utensils, etc., that Alfred brought in)*: And all of this?
ALFRED: Oupa's things.
VERONICA: Oh my God! . . . yes! I remember them!

(Alfred grabs his satchel as if to give her something.)

ALFRED: And now . . . uh . . . now . . .
VERONICA: What?

(Alfred wants to tell her something . . .)

ALFRED: . . . You can make this room just like it was.
VERONICA: And I will. You wait and see.

(She looks down at the box of household things.)

This old candleholder . . . it was always on a box next to his bed. There was another one next to my bed. This pot! . . . this old bucket . . .
ALFRED: They was all in here when he died. You know what this village is like. Soon as they heard old Buks Jonkers was dead, they started peeping in through the window to see what he left. The next thing I know is that the window is broken and then I see his clothes walking around even though he is already deep in the ground. No, Alfred, I said. This is not right. Because they are now Veronica's things. One thing he always said to me when we was talking about you and wondering how things was going, "One day she'll come home, Alfred, you wait and see." Just like that. "She will come home." And he was right! Here you are. But you know something else . . . he knew

his end was near. Ja. I know that because one day he gave me a spare key to the door and said that I must look after everything for you just in case. That was all he said. "Just in case." But I knew what he meant. So when I saw that broken window I took everything what was left and kept it at my place. He also told me he gave you a key to the door before you left.

VERONICA: Here it is. *(She shows the padlock key on a little chain around her neck)* My lucky charm.

ALFRED: But why did it take you so long to come back?

VERONICA: I don't know. You know how it is, man—you get busy and so put things off until tomorrow . . . and then when tomorrow comes it's now today . . . so you put it off again . . . and so it goes.

(Pause. Veronica is embarrassed by her feeble attempts to avoid Alfred's question.)

I'm being stupid. Why did I wait so long to come back? *(Looking around at the room)* I was scared.

ALFRED: Of what?

VERONICA: Of being in here. Of the ghosts waiting for me in here.

ALFRED: Spoke?

VERONICA: Yes.

ALFRED: In here?

VERONICA: Ja.

ALFRED: You're joking again.

VERONICA: Wish I was . . . but I'm not. I've already seen them, Alfred. Little Veronica. Oupa. At this table. Eating supper. Playing games with him . . . dreaming about the future . . .

ALFRED: Maybe you saw Oupa. He's dead. But not Veronica. Because how can I see your ghost if you are still alive?

VERONICA: That little Veronica isn't. She's dead. Dead and buried in Cape Town.

ALFRED (*Laughing*): Same old Veronica! You always used to say such funny things. I also believe in ghosts, you know . . . but I haven't seen one yet.

VERONICA: Anyway, to hell with them. Hey? What do you say, Alfred Witbooi?

ALFRED: Ja. I also say to hell with them.

VERONICA: So tell me . . . how did you know I was back already?

ALFRED: I knew you was coming because you said so in your letter, but you didn't say when so I wasn't waiting for you. But then this afternoon Hansie Koekemoer told me you was already here. He said he was in Graaff-Reinet doing some shopping and when he was coming back he saw this woman with a little boy standing by the side of the road waving her thumb for a lift.

VERONICA: He nearly didn't stop.

ALFRED: Ja. That's what he said. But after he passed you he thought, "No, wait now. I know this woman." He looked again in the mirror and then it comes to him: "Veronica! Veronica Jonkers!" He said it just like that: "Veronica Jonkers is back, Alfred."

VERONICA: Haai . . . I'm telling you . . . when I saw that old flenter bakkie stop and go into reverse and who it was sitting in there driving it . . . I said, "Thank you, God."

We were moeg, Alfred. Moeg, moeg, moeg! But let me tell you, it's the same old baasie—even though he is old enough now for his grave, his hand kept missing the gears and grabbing my knee! (*Laughter*)

ALFRED: So is that how you come all the way from Cape Town—thumb in the wind?

VERONICA: No, man! Give us a break! First it was the train to P.E. Then only did we start standing on the side of the road. It wasn't too bad. There's still some soft hearts left in this world—'specially when they saw the little boy standing with me.

ALFRED: And now here you are. For how long?

VERONICA: What do you mean "how long?" Forever. This is permanent occupation.

ALFRED: This is now going to be home?

VERONICA: Yes! I've come home, man. To stay! *(She sits at the table)*

ALFRED: Didn't you have one in Cape Town?

VERONICA: Not what I would call "home." Places to live and sleep . . . some of them okay, some of them not so okay . . . but not home like this was . . . and is going to be! . . . Not so, Mannetjie? We are going to make this a real home. Come, my darling . . . come sit here with Mommy.

(Mannetjie joins his mother at the table.)

So your first job, Alfred Witbooi, is to help me find work. Ja! Don't look so surprised. I got to earn a living like everybody else.

ALFRED: What sort of work?

VERONICA: Ag, come on Alfred! You know. House cleaning, washing . . . that sort of thing. Make inquiries. Ja. I know what you're thinking. Doesn't sound like the little Veronica who said she wasn't going to scrub floors, hey. Well, like I said, she is dead and buried. This Veronica who's talking to you now has got a hungry little mouth in her life that needs a lot of food.

ALFRED *(Gesturing to Mannetjie)*: So is it yours?

VERONICA: Hey! Watch your language, please. He is not just a "it." He's my son and he's got a name just like you. His proper name is Manfred Jonkers. *(To Mannetjie)* My darling, I want you to meet Mr. Alfred Witbooi. He is a very good friend, darling, so you must say hello to him.

ALFRED: Hello. Mannetjie.

(Alfred waits but Mannetjie just stares at him.)

VERONICA: He's shy . . . and clever. He can already read some words . . . not so, Mannetjie?

ALFRED: Who was his pa?

VERONICA: Manfred Mannyike.

ALFRED: A black man? Not a Colored man? Bantu?

VERONICA *(Defiantly)*: Yes! Bantu. He's a black man and a good man. Anything wrong with that?

ALFRED *(Remembers Veronica's temper)*: No . . . no . . . I was just asking.

VERONICA: Well, now you know.

ALFRED: Please, man! I didn't mean anything bad. Truly.

VERONICA *(Relenting)*: I know, I know. You are Alfred Witbooi and that is how you were and always will be. No manners.

ALFRED *(Eagerly—happy to have escaped her wrath)*: Yes, that is how I am! No manners. So tell me . . . what was it like down there in Cape Town?

VERONICA *(Defensively)*: Okay. You know . . .

ALFRED: Good times!

VERONICA *(Evasively)*: That's right. Good times. Plenty of good times.

ALFRED: Lots of singing.

VERONICA: Lots of singing. But what about you? Tell me your news.

ALFRED: I got no news.

VERONICA: Don't be silly. Of course you got news. Everybody's got some news. Are you married?

ALFRED: To who?

VERONICA: Anybody. Have you got a wife, for God's sake?

ALFRED: Never!

VERONICA: No children?

ALFRED: Not that I know of.

VERONICA: Have you at least got a girlfriend?

ALFRED: My ma says I don't need one. But she's going to die soon I think, so who know! Maybe something will happen.

VERONICA (*Sad little laugh and a shake of head*): Ja, definitely still the same old Alfred, hey. Did you ever get that bicycle you was always dreaming about?

ALFRED: Maybe.

VERONICA: What do you mean "maybe"? You got it or you didn't. Have you got money?

ALFRED (*Warily*): Yes. There is . . . there is some money.

VERONICA: So you are saving.

ALFRED: That's it. I'm saving.

(*He is not a very good liar.*)

VERONICA: You're looking skelm, Alfred! What you hiding?

ALFRED: Nothing.

VERONICA (*A little laugh and shake of her head*): I made up a song about you, you know. You and that bicycle.

ALFRED: You did? Sing it for me.

VERONICA (*Dismissively*): Ag, it's not so special.

ALFRED: Come on, man! That's not like you. You always wanted to sing.

VERONICA (*Laughing*): All right, all right. I'll give you a little bit of it.

(*With Mannetjie on her lap she sings halfheartedly:*)

Wake up! Wake up!
Alfred Witbooi!
Wake up! Wake up!
And dream properly.
Dream big!
Dream grand!
Don't let your life be secondhand . . .

. . . And so on.

ALFRED: Hey, I like it! But do it now properly . . . the way you use to. Remember? Like it was a concert.

(Veronica tries to protest but at the same time it is obvious that she is tempted to go along with Alfred. In the meantime, Alfred has found a wooden box and has positioned it for Veronica's performance.)

Big crowd of people! Veronica Jonkers is tops of the pops! Number one on the hit parade! *(To Mannetjie)* You must also be the crowd. Okay? So when I clap and shout you must also clap and shout. *(Back to Veronica)* Now remember . . . we paid a lot of money for the concert. Okay, you ready? Here we go . . .

(He launches the concert with hand clapping, feet stomping and shouting. After a hesitant start, Mannetjie also goes for it full throttle.)

ALFRED AND MANNETJIE: We want Veronica! We want Veronica!
VERONICA *(Now caught up in the game)*: Thank you . . . thank you . . . thank you. I am now going to sing you a song about my good friend Alfred Witbooi.

(More shouts and cheers from the crowd.)

His dream was to have his own bicycle but because we was all so poor all he could dream about was the broken old secondhand bicycle that Baasie Koopman wanted to sell.

(She launches into the song, going for it full blast. At the end of it, the "crowd" goes wild.)

> Wake up! Wake up!
> Alfred Witbooi!
> Wake up! Wake up!
> And dream properly.
> Dream big!

Dream grand!
Don't let you life be secondhand.
Live it big!
Live it grand!
So wake up, wake up!
Alfred Witbooi!
You can have that bike,
Any way you like.
Just wake up, wake up!
And dream properly.
Alfred Witbooi!

(A laughing and adrenalized Veronica steps off the stage.)

Hell . . . but I enjoyed that!

ALFRED: Me, too. But you want to know something . . . I just seen my first ghost.

VERONICA: What do you mean?

ALFRED: The young Veronica. That was her doing all the singing, you know. Maybe she is not so dead after all . . . hey?

(Veronica laughs happily.)

VERONICA *(To Mannetjie)*: Did you like it, my darling?

MANNETJIE: Yes.

VERONICA: I also use to give Oupa concerts like that in here. But it was very hard with him because he wasn't a good crowd like Alfred and you. His favorite songs were always the ones I use to make about him and his akkers . . . you know . . . the rain, the vegetables, the fruit tree flowers . . . all those things. You can't really get the crowd going with songs about potatoes and pumpkins.

ALFRED: Ja. Oupa and his akkers, hey. That was his life . . . his akkers and you. I look after them now.

VERONICA: You do?

ALFRED: Ja. He made me his partner. When his hands got very bad with the rumatiek and he couldn't hold the spade properly anymore. It was after you had gone to Cape Town. I was just walking up there past the akkers one morning. You know what it was like . . . you got nothing to do so you just walk around because maybe something will happen. He sees me standing there in the road watching him so he calls to me to come to him. The master had given him two small fig trees to plant but his hands were so stiff and sore that day he couldn't dig the hole properly. So I did. Ja . . . those two little trees are big now. Just last week I picked figs from them. Anyway, next time it was to help him set up tralies for his beans; then leading water, and so on.

I did all that for him. Then one day he said I must work with him full time. I asked my ma and she said it was okay because I wouldn't get work anywhere else. I was too dom, she said. (*Little laugh*) Ma is always making jokes like that. So there we were: Oupa sitting under the walnut tree teaching me how I must plant potatoes and carrots and cabbages, and be careful of the frost, and when to lead water. You know, sometimes now when I'm working there on the akkers it feels like his spook is sitting there under the walnut tree watching me, telling me I'm doing it wrong, that I must do it this way or that way. (*Tapping his head*) All the things he knew is now here in my head. But also you. More and more we also talked about you, Veronica. What is she doing? Is she singing? Is she okay? It was my job to go to the post office every Saturday to ask if there was a letter from you.

VERONICA (*Defensively*): I did write.

ALFRED: Four letters.

(*He goes to his sling bag and takes out four letters, which he brings to the table.*)

Here they are. I been keeping them for you. First this one, then this one, then this one . . . but not this one. He was already gone when it came. I didn't open it.

(He offers them to Veronica. She shakes her head. Alfred leaves them on the table.)

The day when there was a letter we did almost no work. First I had to go find Hansie Kloppers to read the letters for us. Remember him? He was almost as good as you in school. Then we would all sit under the walnut tree and listen to Hansie reading them. And not just once! "Again," Oupa would say to him. "Again." And then, "Again." And then the questions. "Does she say where she is living now?" "Does she say she has found work?" You see, Oupa didn't believe Hansie was reading everything in the letter so he would argue with him, telling him he was cheating and that he didn't read everything because why didn't Veronica say where she was living now and what she was eating . . . and all the things that Oupa wanted to know. And then Hansie would get the hell in and tell Oupa not to ask him to read any more letters, and walk off. Me and Oupa would go on sitting there, with Oupa talking to the letter as if it was going to speak to him and answer all his questions. That is where he died, you know. Ja. You see, there was one terrible winter here. I never known cold like that. Every day, every night. Snow on all the mountains. Oupa's bones was so cold he couldn't get out of the bed some mornings. I was sure he was going to go that winter. But he didn't. Your oupa was biltong, Veronica, because when it started to get warm again there he was on the akkers planting pumpkins. But you know, one day it looked to me like something had happened to him, something in him had died that winter. I don't know what, but he just stopped talking . . . Ja, even about you.

Another day, he was sitting there while I was planting some more pumpkin seeds—a late frost had killed off all our first small ones—and I just thought he had gone to sleep again because more and more he use to sleep there under the tree while I worked. But when it was time to rest and eat our bread I stopped working and went there to sit with him. He opened his eyes and was looking at me and I was telling him how one little pumpkin plant hadn't been killed by the frost. He smiled, Veronica . . . so waar! Not a big one but his eyes crinkled up the way he use to do it when he was happy. It looked like he was going to say something, but then he closed them again and this time I knew it wasn't sleep. Oupa was gone. So the police sergeant came and looked at him, and then sister from the clinic, and they all said he was dead. So that is how it was.

VERONICA: As soon as I got things organized in here you must bring me some flowers and take me and Mannetjie to his grave.

ALFRED: I can't.

VERONICA: Why not?

ALFRED: There's no grave, Veronica. Ja. It's gone! The big storm we had. Didn't you know about it? It was on the wireless. Gatsrivier in flood. We couldn't get out of the valley for two weeks. It was so bad the dam up in the kloof broke open and the water rushed down and washed away half of our graveyard. That is where Oupa was buried.

It was terrible! All the coffins broke open . . . bones and skeletons of the dead people was lying everywhere in the veld. The jackals came and carried away half of them. We collected as many as possible and laid them out on the ground in that old garage next to the police station, but the trouble was nobody could tell what bones was belonging to what dead person. So then the arguments started. Somebody would pick up a bone and say, "This is my old Auntie Kootie," and then somebody else jumps in

and says, "No, it isn't. It's my father . . . old Jannie Engel-
brecht!" . . . and so on. It ended up with a big meeting
where we all decided it was better to dig just one big hole
and bury them all in it. I'll take you to that, if you like.

*(A long pause as Veronica struggles to deal with her emotions.
She holds her little son close. Alfred watches.)*

Your little outjie is fast asleep. *(Yawns)* Me also. I must go
now. My ma will be worried about me. She doesn't like me
to be out when it gets dark. *(Moving to go)* So listen . . . I'll
bring you some vegetables tomorrow after my work. I got
some nice cabbages and tomatoes this year.

*(Veronica nods and murmurs a soft, "Thank you, Alfred."
  He leaves. She then carries the sleeping Mannetjie to the bed
and takes off his shoes before covering him with a blanket. She
sits at his bedside gently smoothing the hair on his head. After
a few seconds she can no longer control her turbulent emotions.)*

VERONICA *(Stifling sobs)*: I'm sorry, Mannetjie. Mommy is so . . .
so . . . sorry. I promise I will try to make it right for you.
But please forgive her. That is all she can hope for now . . .
that one day you will understand and forgive her.

*(It is now getting dark in the room. Veronica goes to the table
where she sets up and lights a candle that Alfred brought. The
four letters she wrote Oupa lie in front of her on the table, the
unopened one on top. After a few seconds of hesitation, she picks
it up and reads the address:)*

Mr. Abraam Jonkers,
    Post Office—Nieu Bethesda,
    Graaff-Reinet District,
    Cape Province.

(While Veronica looks at the envelope, Oupa enters through the door. He is the figure of a tired old man. He closes the door, takes off his hat and puts his spade down. He turns to Veronica and looks at her. She looks at him.)

What's the matter, Oupa? Why are you looking at me like that?

OUPA *(Directly to her)*: Memories, my child. It's all the memories. You are too young still to have any, but one day you will have your own. Some of them will make you happy, some of them will make you sad.

Like the day I was working here on the akkers when Alfred came running to me with a message that your Ouma Betty had phoned from Graaff-Reinet to say I must meet the railway bus. You see, we had gotten a message from Johannesburg to say your mother, Caroline, was very sick, and your ouma had gone up to be there with her. So when I got the message to meet the bus, I thought she was bringing your mother back. No one said anything to us about a baby, but instead of your mother, it was you, Veronica. By the time your Ouma Betty got to the hospital, your mother had died. Betty never saw her daughter again.

After your ouma got off the bus and we were walking home—I was carrying her suitcase and she was carrying you—you started to cry. And I thought, "Oh, heavens, this child is going to be difficult, I can hear that right now." And I said so to your ouma. But she said, "No, Buks. She's not crying. She's singing. She's singing, Buks." She said. "Look for yourself." And I did . . . and so waar! . . . I could see she was right. You know the way a baby squashes and wrinkles up its face when it's crying, like a dirty old handkerchief you've been sneezing in the whole summer, well, that wasn't what I saw. Your eyes were open, your face was smooth and this funny little noise was bubbling out of your mouth . . . Betty was right! You were singing. And so it was from then on. Your ouma always used to say to me, "If that child ever stops singing, Abraam Yonkers, then you must know there is something wrong with the world."

VERONICA: So do you understand now, Oupa? Why I want to go?

OUPA: No, I don't.

VERONICA: But you just said it, Oupa. I have to sing.

OUPA: So sing. Nobody is stopping you.

VERONICA: No. Oupa doesn't understand.

OUPA: Then you must explain it to me.

VERONICA: I want to sing to lots of people.

OUPA: But you already do that. In church. At the school concert. You know how much everybody likes your singing and all the nice songs you make.

VERONICA: That's not enough.

OUPA: Not enough? I hear you. The whole village hears you. God hears you. And that is not enough?

VERONICA: I don't mean it that way, Oupa. But I don't just want to sing hymns and the same old school songs to the same old people . . . over and over again.

OUPA: But you don't. Every time I listen there's a new song coming out of you.

VERONICA: You mean the ones I make up myself?

OUPA: Ja. And let me tell you, my girl, those are the best songs I ever heard.

VERONICA: Oupa is just saying that to make me happy.

OUPA: If it makes you happy that's good—but I'm saying it because it's the truth.

VERONICA: I made a new one this morning when I was cleaning the house. So do you want to hear it?

OUPA: But of course.

VERONICA: Are you ready?

OUPA: Yes. I'm ready.

VERONICA: It's called "Oupa and Veronica."

(She sings the song with uninhibited energy and joy:)

You plant seeds,
And I sing songs.
We're Oupa and Veronica,
Yes, Oupa and Veronica.

You work hard,
And I dream dreams.
That's Oupa and Veronica,
Yes, Oupa and Veronica.

Summer into autumn,
Winter into spring,
Planting seeds and singing songs.
That's Oupa and Veronica,
Yes, Oupa and Veronica.

But one happy day,
I must go away,
And you must stay.
Because we're Oupa and Veronica.

While you are planting seeds,
I'll be singing my songs,
In places far away.
'Cause you're Oupa and I'm Veronica.

(During the last two verses, Oupa picks up his hat and spade and leaves. Veronica is so caught up in her song that she doesn't register his departure until the end. Flushed with excitement, she turns to where Oupa was standing.)

So do you like it? . . . Oupa? Oupa?

(The scene slowly segues back to reality: Veronica is alone, but for her sleeping child.)

Act Two

SCENE 1

The same room a few years later. It is now a warm lived-in space with a colorful cover on the bed, bright floral curtains for the window and corner space, and a plastic cloth on the table. There are also pictures on the wall—mostly unframed cutouts from magazines and newspapers. The little shelf with Oupa's tins of seed is now shared by a small collection of books. The tin mug still hangs from its nail.

A small battery-powered radio on the table is playing a pop tune and an overload of crackling static.

Veronica is alone and is listlessly preparing for a meal—laying out plates and spoons on the table. She is obviously not well and is also worried. She has to sit down to rest and think.

She is pulled out of her reverie by a knock on the door.

ALFRED'S VOICE: Just me, Veronica. Can I come in?

VERONICA: Yes.

(Alfred enters. He hangs up his old canvas bag—a habitual action whenever he enters—then eyes Veronica. He cautiously

79

approaches the table. He brings over a plastic bag of vegetables and tries hard to sound and behave as casually as possible.)

ALFRED: Somebody left the oven door open again today. Shoo! . . . but it's hot out there. But it looks like a thunderstorm might be on the way.

(Pause.)

How you feeling?

VERONICA: Okay.

(Alfred is not convinced.)

I said I'm okay.

ALFRED: Good. Ja . . . that's good! *(Unpacking the vegetables)* Nice cabbage and a few of the last carrots. If it stays hot like this it won't be long before the pumpkins will be ready. *(Mimicking Oupa's voice)* "Flat white Boer Pampoen!" Remember?

VERONICA: Oupa.

ALFRED: Ja. Oupa. His favorite. *(Looking around)* Where's Mannetjie?

VERONICA: Still at school. He's helping the new teacher, Miss Viljoen, with something. I think he's her favorite. Ja. It's always Miss Viljoen wants this or Miss Viljoen wants that.

ALFRED: Because he's clever.

VERONICA *(Proudly)*: He knows all the words in his schoolbooks. Spells them right as well. There's even some words I don't know.

ALFRED: Me, also. I was okay at counting, remember, but not reading and writing? I tried hard there in the classroom but I could never get the big words right. And then what is the difference between a verb and a noun. No, thank you!

VERONICA: "Okay at counting"? You were useless, man. I was cheating for you all the time. All you ever tried hard to do was get a ride on somebody's bicycle.

ALFRED: Because I didn't have my own one. Anyway, when somebody did lend me theirs I always gave you plenty of rides on the handlebars.

VERONICA: Ja, you did . . . and also plenty of scabs on my legs when you crashed into something and I fell off.

ALFRED: Because you wouldn't listen to me and sit still. Waving at everybody and singing! I couldn't steer straight.

(Forced laughter from Alfred. He is trying very hard to cheer her up.)

Those were happy days, hey Veronica? You know, sometimes I just sit and do nothing and remember all the things we did. This morning I was remembering the church picnics. Those were now really big fun! Riding out to van Heerden's farm in the trailer behind the tractor! Singing hymns all the way when we was going along. And what about the races? The stone and spoon race when you had to run without dropping it.

(Picks up a spoon from the table and demonstrates.)

VERONICA *(He is beginning to get on her nerves)*: Okay, Alfred.

ALFRED: But your best was always the sack race. I can still see you: "On your marks! Get set! Go!"

(Carried away, he launches into another demonstration—this time cavorting and leaping around the room like a kangaroo.
Veronica, who up until now has tried politely to endure Alfred's antics, can now not take any more.)

VERONICA: For God's sake, Alfred, stop now! What's the matter with you, man? Three years since I've been back,

"Remember this! Remember that!" Is that all you got in your head? Stupid bloody memories? Ja. Stupid and useless. They're good for nothing. I wish to God I didn't have any. Because if you think they can make me happy, you got another guess coming. That little Veronica winning the sack race was a bloody fool. Yes! A fool. She didn't know what this world is really like. I do!

(Her outburst has left her exhausted and coughing violently. An alarmed and helpless Alfred watches her silently. When the coughing fit passes, she turns to Alfred with a helpless gesture.)

I'm sorry, Alfred . . . I'm not cross with you. I know you mean good. It's me I hate.

ALFRED: No, man . . . you don't have to say sorry to me! It's okay if you get cross. I know I get on people's nerves.

VERONICA: The only person I am cross with is myself. Truly, man, that little Veronica was not as clever as you think. She should have known that all those "happy memories" were just a trick . . . and they fooled her all right.

ALFRED: It's no good to say things like that. You are sick.

VERONICA: That's right. I'm sick.

ALFRED *(Summoning up courage for a confrontation)*: So then listen to me now. This is really no good, Veronica. You have got to go to the clinic. I'll go with you. Sister Cornelius must have something there on the shelf that can help you.

VERONICA *(Shaking her head vigorously)*: No . . . No! . . .

ALFRED: Then let me get you a lift from somebody into Graaff-Reinet and go and see the nurses at the hospital or even the chemist shop. They get lots of medicines from Port Elizabeth. Maybe that new medicine we heard about on the wireless is down there.

VERONICA: I said *no*! For God's sake, Alfred, are you now so dom that you don't even understand the word "no"? All I need is rest. What I'm suffering from is . . . is exhaustion.

So let us just leave it at that. And for God's sake don't talk about it to anybody. I don't want the people in the village skinnering about me. If they ask you about me you must tell them I got a very bad flu.

ALFRED: Okay. *(Not at all convinced)* But it's not the flu, hey.

VERONICA: No.

ALFRED: It's something else, hey. *(Veronica is now too exhausted to argue anymore)* Something very bad. *(He waits. Veronica says nothing)* Haai, Veronica! Is it . . . you know . . .

VERONICA: What? *(She knows what he means)* Go on. Don't be frightened. Say it! You won't catch it if you just say its name. *(Pause)* So must I say it for you? "Is it AIDS?"

(She throttles a surge of emotion.)

Yes. It's AIDS.

ALFRED: Oh, my God.

VERONICA: Terrible, hey! Now you're really frightened. Ag . . . to hell with you. Just go. Get the hell out and go and don't come back. Mannetjie and I don't need you.

(She leaves the table and goes to sit on the bed. Alfred doesn't move.)

So? What you waiting for?

ALFRED: Please don't be like that. Help me. What can I do . . . for you. I don't know anything about it.

(He waits. Veronica is having a hard time controlling her emotions. Eventually . . .)

VERONICA: Just be my friend.

ALFRED: But I am.

VERONICA: I know you are.

(Alfred waits for advice.)

83

Please . . . you mustn't say anything about it . . . to anybody. I'm a good actress. I've kept it for three years and
you keep it that way. So you understand?

ALFRED: Yes.

VERONICA: Say you won't.

ALFRED: I won't what?

VERONICA: For God's sake, Alfred . . . that you won't tell anybody.

ALFRED: Okay, okay! I won't. I promise I won't. But what about
Mrs. Conradie. She asked me yesterday when you coming
back to work.

VERONICA: Say it's very bad flu and I don't want her to catch it.
She must get somebody else to clean for her. Say the doctor in Graaff-Reinet said I must rest for a long time. That
is what you must tell everybody. Because you know what
this village is like. How people skinner about each other.
And they got all the wrong ideas about it. Ja. You also.
I can see it in your eyes Alfred. "Can I catch it from her?"
Not so? "If I eat the food she cooks will I catch it?" "If she
sneezes will I catch it?" Don't shake your head. I can see
it! It will be the same out there. The next thing you know,
if they find out about me, is mommies are telling their
children they mustn't play with Mannetjie. Next thing is
the teachers don't want him in the classroom. I know how
to fool people, so you keep your mouth shut.

ALFRED (*Horrified*): Has he also got it?

(*A pause . . . Then Veronica explodes.*)

VERONICA (*Violently . . . barely restraining the impulse to hit him*):
Fuck you, Alfred Witbooi! Fuck you!! What sort of mother
do you think I am? Do you think we would be here if he
also had it? We'd both be dead . . . and it wouldn't be the
AIDS that did it. Me. Yes . . . I would do it. Both of us
together. Carry him to the railway line like a woman I knew

and stand there and wait for the train. That's what she did. Stood there with her three children waiting for the train to kill them all. And it did. So fuck you again, Alfred Witbooi. What you waiting for? Get the hell out.

(Pause. Once again Alfred doesn't move.)

The answer to your question is "no." Mannetjie is as clean and sweet as the day he was born, thank God.

(Veronica breaks down, her body shaking as she tries to control her sobbing. Alfred approaches her uncertainly.)

ALFRED: I'm sorry. Please don't cry. I didn't mean to hurt you . . . or Mannetjie. Just remember . . . I don't know about these things. Please stop now. I won't tell anybody what you told me and I won't say anything about it in here. Veronica? Please stop now. And . . . listen to me . . . I will go if you want me to. You mustn't let Mannetjie see you like this. He's coming back from school soon.

VERONICA *(Gradually calming down)*: Mannetjie was born before I got it. Do you understand, Alfred? He was already three years old when I . . . oh my God! I hate myself. Every night I pray that he won't also hate me . . . one day when he finds out about his mommy.

ALFRED: He won't, Veronica. You are his mommy. He loves you. Children always love their mommies. Even me. I didn't know it until she was dead. But then I cried. *(Pause)* But . . . I mean . . . how? What happened there in Cape Town?

VERONICA: Do you really want to know?

ALFRED: Is it bad?

VERONICA: Yes. It's bad.

ALFRED: Then maybe no. I don't want to hear it.

VERONICA: Too late! I can't keep it inside me any longer. I got nobody else but you.

(The following is a moment that demands the truth, and she tells it simply, without any emotional adornment.)

Oh God, where do I begin? Cape Town! What I wrote to Oupa in those letters was all just lies. I was ashamed of myself for doing it, but I didn't want to upset him, you see. That is why I stopped writing. There was a time when it looked like it was all going to be all right and have a happy ending. Because I ended up working at the Holiday Inn there by the airport, you know, cleaning the rooms and that sort of thing. It wasn't little Veronica's dream come true but it was a good job, Alfred. Good pay. Took me a long time to get that one. Before then I was doing all sorts of odd jobs. Anything I could find. Because, let me tell you now: things was not easy down there. It wasn't anything like I thought it was going to be. You see, my Uncle Dawie, who I was staying with, wasn't a nice man. Every Friday night he got drunk. My Auntie Lena—his wife—said I must get out of the house or hide somewhere because when he was like that he was full of nonsense and did bad things with young girls.

If it wasn't for Debsie I would have come back here a lot earlier! She was my best friend. Debsie Janse. Lived two houses down the road. Boy! . . . She helped me a lot. We used to go out and do things together. One day I told her about my dream to be a singer. She said it was a good idea, and took me to a shebeen and told me to sing for the customers. At first I was too shy but she pushed until I did sing. I still remember: it was "Deep in the Heart of Texas."

ALFRED: Ja. That was my favorite! Remember? You made me clap my hands with you.

(Tries to sing:)

The stars are bright . . .

(He claps.)

Deep in the heart of Texas.

VERONICA: Yes . . . they also liked it there in the shebeen. So
the next thing is this black guy comes and sits next to me
and Debsie and buys us a drink.

ALFRED: You was drinking?

VERONICA: Just sipping it . . . at first. You got to. You can't say
no to those guys . . . Anyway . . . His name was Manfred.
Manfred Mannyike. We got talking and when I told him
I was looking for a job, he said I must come to him at the
Holiday Inn, where he was working. He said they were
looking for girls to clean the rooms and he would take
me straight to the manager. And there it was at last . . . a
real job, and good pay. It was some time before Manfred
and me got really serious with each other. He kept trying,
but I said no. But that didn't stop him. You see, he said it
was true love and he was falling head over heels for me.
Showed me the condoms the government was giving away
for free. Promised me we would get married afterwards.
So we got engaged. That's the way it works down there.
You get engaged and then it's okay for the two of you. But
that was the end of my good luck. Manfred got killed one
night in a fight in that same shebeen where we first met.

ALFRED: What happened?

VERONICA: I don't really know. I wasn't with him at the time.
But the people that was there in the shebeen told me the
fight was all because Manfred wasn't a real South African.
You see, he came from Mozambique. That night one other
guy in the shebeen was very drunk and said Manfred had
no right to be in the country and that he was taking jobs
away from real South Africans. Manfred wasn't scared
of nobody, you see, so he got cross and told this other
guy that it was maybe because people from Mozambique

was cleverer than "real South Africans" . . . and then the knives came out. Ja. That's what it's like down there. Cape Town! The devil made that place, Alfred, not God. Not long afterwards I started feeling sick—you know, vomiting and all that—and when I told one of the other girls, she said it sounded like I was pregnant. She was right. Mannetjie was on the way. Those government condoms was rotten and no good.

ALFRED: So that's who his father is.

VERONICA: Yes, of course. There was nobody else . . . that time. *(Defensively)* And he was clean, Alfred! I can see what's going on in your head and you are wrong. Manfred was a good man and a clean man. He was always warning me about it, and saying both of us must be very careful. Anyway . . . from then on, it was just one thing after another.

You see, I was getting big with Mannetjie. I tried to hide it at first but the little donner just kept growing inside me. Then one day the manager called me to his office and said it wouldn't look good for business, so I lost my job. And then I was kicked out of the place where I was staying . . . I couldn't pay the rent, you see . . . and then . . .

(She pauses, ashamed of what she was on the point of telling him. After a few seconds she continues:)

Ag to hell with it . . . I may as well tell you. I really started drinking—and from then on it was just, like they say, downhill. *(Bitterly)* We ended up in a squatter camp on the Cape Flats. Lots of "nice" men there! They all wanted to buy me a drink and help little Veronica and her baby. Ja! That's how it was. The next thing I know is that I got it . . . the AIDS . . . engagement present from one of those nice men. Bastards! But what really frightened me then is that a woman there said that when child welfare heard about me having AIDS, they would take my baby away, because that is what they did to a friend of hers. That was it. All I had to live for was that little chap. If I lost him then I would really be gone. It sobered me up, Alfred! Like that! *(Clicks her fingers)* That same night I said no to a "very nice man" and his bottle. I told him to go to hell and I sat there in that miserable little pondok with Mannetjie in my arms. The whole night . . . awake . . . just me and him and a lot of questions! What has happened to you, Veronica Jonkers? What are you going to do? Do you want to lose him? What would Oupa say if he saw you now? I won't ever forget that night . . . But at the end of it I had a plan. I borrowed a little bit here, a little bit there, and when I had enough, Mannetjie and I were sitting on the train to P.E. I haven't had a drink since.

ALFRED: This . . . this AIDS . . . is it like they say . . . you know . . . serious?

VERONICA: Yes, Alfred. It's very serious.

ALFRED: Isn't there medicines for it?

VERONICA: Yes there is, but it costs a hell of a lot of money and the government says it's too expensive to give to the poor people for free. We must just eat bananas and buy vitamin pills.

(Alfred turns from Veronica, surreptitiously carrying his shoulder bag.)

ALFRED: How much does it cost, Veronica?

VERONICA: What?

ALFRED: The medicines.

VERONICA: Oh, Alfred, you don't want to know.

ALFRED: One hundred rand?

VERONICA: Don't be stupid, Alfred. They cost hundreds and hundreds of rands, every month. Because you have to take medicines every month for as long as you live.

ALFRED: So, it's big. So it's like thousands and thousands of rands?

VERONICA: Yes. Many, many thousands, Alfred.

ALFRED: So . . . what's going to happen? I mean . . . how long? . . .

(He is struggling with the unspeakable.)

VERONICA: It's okay, Alfred. I know what you mean. Sometimes it's very quick, sometimes very slow . . . but nobody gets better. It's there in you for keeps.

ALFRED: So what you going to do, Veronica? About Mannetjie and everything . . .

VERONICA: I got a plan.

ALFRED: Good. You got a plan.

VERONICA: Oh, yes . . . and I think it's a good one.

ALFRED: That's very good. What is your plan?

VERONICA: You.

ALFRED: I'm your plan?

VERONICA: Yes. You're going to marry me.

ALFRED: Veronica?

VERONICA: You heard me right. You're going to marry me.

ALFRED *(Dumbfounded)*: Since when?

VERONICA: Since now.

ALFRED: You're making a joke.

VERONICA: God, how I wish I was! But this is serious. I've never been more serious in all my life.

(Alfred shakes his head in denial. He wants to speak, but Veronica won't let him.)

No. Don't say anything. Just listen. It's not for me. I don't want you in my bed, so don't be frightened about that. It's for Mannetjie. Don't you see? What's going to happen to him when I'm gone? He's still so small! I'm not going to get better. Ja. This is it. When I go, child welfare will come to grab him and there won't be anybody to stop them and say, "No, you can't do that. I am his daddy. He stays with me." He's got to have somebody to protect him, and when you marry me . . . yes, you are going to! . . . When you marry me, you will be able to do that. Not so? Like I said, it's not for me. Nothing will happen between us. It's for that little Outjie, Alfred. You got nothing to lose. You got nobody in your life anymore. Your ma is dead. It's too late now to get any woman to go with you.

ALFRED: But he doesn't like me! You know that.

VERONICA: He will. You must teach him.

ALFRED: I don't know how to teach somebody to like me. The only persons who did was my ma. And you. Because you do like me, don't you?

VERONICA: Yes I do . . . and so will Mannetjie. I know how you must do it. I'll give you some good tips. First one is be patient with him, Alfred. He's still only a little boy, remember. Just talk to him nicely like everything was all right between the two of you. Even if he is rude to you, don't you be rude to him. Just pretend it's okay between you and him. And tell him stories. He likes stories. 'Specially about me and Oupa. That is a big promise you must make to him. Please don't let him forget me! Please, Alfred . . .

(Veronica is on the verge of breaking down but, before that can happen, the front door opens and an excited Mannetjie bursts into the room. He holds up a book proudly.)

MANNETJIE: Mommy! Mommy! Look at what Miss Viljoen gave me.

VERONICA *(Reading the title)*: *Karoo and Other Stories*. Now I wonder why she gave you that. You are mos a naughty boy, not so?

MANNETJIE: No, I'm not.

ALFRED *(Trying to speak nicely)*: Your mommy is only joking, Mannetjie. She doesn't mean it.

MANNETJIE *(Angrily)*: You don't know nothing about me and my mommy.

ALFRED *(Turning to Veronica with a helpless gesture)*: See! There you have it.

VERONICA *(Ignoring him)*: Read us some of it while I get the supper ready, Bokkie.

MANNETJIE *(Putting away his book)*: No.

(He goes and sits on his bed.)

VERONICA: Ag, come now! Why not? Don't be shy. We won't laugh if you make some mistakes. Not so, Alfred?

MANNETJIE: I won't make any mistakes. I read it to Miss Viljoen and I didn't make any mistakes.

VERONICA: That's wonderful, my darling, but now please read us a little bit as well.

MANNETJIE: No, not now. I'll read to you when he's gone.

VERONICA: Alfred is not just a him, Mannetjie! Remember our manners, please.

ALFRED: I don't care if he doesn't want to read to me! Ja. Go ahead and read to your ma because I am going.

VERONICA: You are going nowhere. Stay right where you are, Alfred Witbooi!

(Steadies herself and then goes and sits beside Mannetjie on the bed.)

Come now, darling. We don't want to fight with each other, 'specially because I got a big surprise for you.

(Mannetjie looks expectantly at her.)

Yes . . . a big surprise. You ready for it?

MANNETJIE: Yes.

VERONICA: You know how you are always asking me about your daddy?

MANNETJIE: Yes.

VERONICA: Well, you know I can't bring him back to you because he is living with the angels now. So I've got a new one for you.

(Pause. Mannetjie waits. She points at Alfred.)

Him. *(Turning to Alfred)* Sit down, Alfred, and tell Mannetjie what you are going to do to me.

ALFRED: No, Veronica. Please.

VERONICA: Yes, Alfred . . . and thank you. I accept. *(To Mannetjie)* Mr. Witbooi has proposed to me. He is going to marry me.

MANNETJIE: Him?

VERONICA: Yes. He is going to be your new stepdaddy.

MANNETJIE: I don't want him for a daddy, Mommy.

ALFRED: And I don't want you!

MANNETJIE: He is so stupid, Mommy! He can't do anything.

ALFRED: Listen to him. And you want me to be his stepdaddy. He is too big for his boots. Go get me a baboon rather for a stepson.

(For a few minutes, a grimly determined Veronica endures the verbal fireworks between the other two as they try to outdo each other with insults. When it doesn't stop, she takes control and silences them.)

VERONICA: Just shut up, both of you!! I've had enough nonsense tonight. Now listen carefully, both of you. *(To Alfred)* You are going to marry me . . . *(To Mannetjie)* . . . And he is going to be your stepdaddy, and both of you will treat each other with good manners. Finish and klaar. Now eat your supper . . . and in case you want the menu, it's bloody bean soup and bread again.

(Mannetjie and Alfred stare balefully at each other as Veronica slices the bread and ladles out the soup.)

Scene 2

Oupa's room, about a year later. Veronica is sitting up in bed. Her condition has deteriorated further. Mannetjie is at her bedside with a bowl of soup. He is trying to feed her with a spoon. He manages to get a few spoonfuls into her mouth before she pushes away his hand.

VERONICA: Please, my darling . . . Mommy is not very hungry today.

MANNETJIE: But you must eat, Mommy. You won't get better if you don't eat.

VERONICA: I will, but later, darling. I promise. So come now, don't look so worried. Mommy really is feeling so much better today. Has Uncle Alfred come back yet?

MANNETJIE: No.

VERONICA: If I'm sleeping when he comes, you must wake me up. Promise?

MANNETJIE: I promise.

(He leaves the bed and goes to the table, where he empties the contents of the bowl back into a pot. Also on the table is Oupa's pumpkin seed tin and an assortment of schoolbooks.)

VERONICA: Mannetjie . . .

MANNETJIE: Yes, Mommy.

VERONICA: Is things getting better between the two of you?

MANNETJIE *(Avoiding her eyes)*: Yes, they are. It's getting better all the time.

VERONICA: Mannetjie . . . are you telling me the truth?

MANNETJIE: Yes, Mommy, it's the truth. We don't fight anymore.

VERONICA: Thank God. That is more important to Mommy than anything else. And please, liefling, when I tell you that he really is now part of our family, you must believe me. I mean, you was there when the magistrate married me and Alfred, weren't you? You heard him say, "I now pronounce you man and wife." That is why Mommy wanted you to be there—so that you could see and hear it happen. I can understand now that you don't want to call him "Daddy." It's okay if he is just "Uncle Alfred" to you. What is important, Mannetjie, is that if anything happens to me, he will be there to look after you.

MANNETJIE: Nothing is going to happen to you, Mommy!

VERONICA: Of course not. Everything is going to be fine. I was just explaining to you about Uncle Alfred. *(Pause)* How was school today?

MANNETJIE: Okay.

VERONICA: Are you still sad about Miss Viljoen leaving?

MANNETJIE: A little bit.

VERONICA: It's like Mommy said, my darling. Miss Viljoen is a nice young lady who also wants to be married and have a wonderful little boy like you. I am sure that one day when you are a big man you will also want to get married. Not so?

MANNETJIE: Yes, Mommy.

VERONICA: And the new teacher? Mr . . . what's his name again?

MANNETJIE: Mr. Arendse.

VERONICA: Is he okay?

MANNETJIE: Yes, Mommy. He's okay.

VERONICA: Just work hard for him the way you did for Miss Viljoen. Then I'm sure he will also try to help us get you into the big school in Graaff-Reinet when the time comes. Uncle Alfred also. He's knows he's got to cook up some good ideas to help us. I know he hasn't got any brains like you, but he is not altogether useless. And he is a good man. So please, my darling, for my sake, and your sake, give him a chance. Okay?

MANNETJIE: Okay.

VERONICA: Now read me some more. Go on with the story about Klonkie. Can you remember where we stopped?

MANNETJIE: Klonkie has found the cave with the bushman paintings at the top of the koppie.

VERONICA: That's right. Go on from there.

MANNETJIE (*Opens one of the books on the table and starts reading, carefully following each word with his forefinger*): "With a pounding heart he now looked carefully around the cave for other signs of the life it had once known but he found nothing. All that remained of that bygone age was those three long-legged red figures racing across the rock face. It was all he needed, though. It was evidence that the cave had once been a home to those people. His people? Yes, his people! He had had thoughts about that when he saw the pictures of them in the book, but now the sense of belonging to them, of being one of them, was final. He couldn't believe his good fortune. He could come up here and make up stories about those three running figures with their bows and arrows whenever he felt like it. He had a secret place all of his own and when he was tired of

making up stories he could just sit up there at the mouth
of the cave and look down at the valley."

(Pause. Mannetjie has a question.)

Mommy? . . .

VERONICA: Yes, darling?

MANNETJIE: How do you make a story?

VERONICA: But you make stories all the time. You are always
telling me stories that you make up.

MANNETJIE: Not like that. I mean like Klonkie. In a book.

VERONICA: The same way, but instead of telling me, you write
it down on paper. And then one day somebody comes and
puts it in a book. Klonkie was first just a story in somebody's head, then he wrote it down on paper. Get the
story in your head first and then write it down on paper
using all your nice big words. Are there any new ones in
what you read Mommy now?

MANNETJIE: Yes. "Pounding." ". . . With a pounding heart."

VERONICA: I think that means Klonkie's heart was beating very
loud.

MANNETJIE: And "bygone age." ". . . All that remained of that
bygone age . . ."

VERONICA: Very long ago.

*(She watches her son as he opens the pumpkin seed tin. Out of
it comes a carefully folded sheet of paper—his list of new words.
He enters the two new ones.)*

How many you got now, Professor?

MANNETJIE: With the two new ones, fifty-seven.

VERONICA: And you still remember what they all mean?

MANNETJIE: Yes. I write it down as well.

(He is very proud of his list, which he now reads aloud. His pronunciation of a few of the longer words is a little strange.)

Devious . . . means "sly," like skelm. Confusion . . . is "all mixed-up." Spon-ta-ne-ous . . . means "all at once." Exit . . . "to leave." Ridicule . . . "to tease somebody and make fun of him." Constant . . . "to be there all the time."

(He looks at his mother. She has fallen asleep. He turns back to his list and goes on reading, but in a softer voice. A few seconds later, Alfred enters quietly. As usual, he hangs up his small sling bag and then joins Mannetjie at the table. He smiles at the boy but gets nothing in return. The open warfare that we last saw between them is now an uneasy armistice. Alfred is obviously trying to make friends, but not Mannetjie. Alfred now listens attentively as Mannetjie reads a few more words from his list.)

Humorous . . . "very funny." Immediate . . . "all at once." In-stan-ta-neo-us . . . "very fast." Fan-tas-tic . . . "very surprising, very strange." Extra-ordinary . . . "also very surprising and strange." Tremendous . . . "very much anything."

(Mannetjie carefully puts the sheet of paper back into the tin.)

ALFRED: Isn't that Oupa's old pumpkin seed tin?
MANNETJIE: Yes, but it's mine now. Mommy said I can have it.
ALFRED: Yes, of course. It's yours. I was just saying, you know.
MANNETJIE: I keep my big words in it.
ALFRED: That's good! Words . . . pumpkin seeds . . . strange world, hey! I also keep my pumpkin seeds in a tin. Ricory coffee tin. I think that one you are holding was an old baking powder tin. Anyway, I'll be planting soon . . . just like Oupa taught me. I think there's no chance of a late frost now and the rain we had is good for planting.

MANNETJIE: Did you go to the clinic and ask about the medicines?

ALFRED: Nothing. Waste of time. Same story as last time. Said I must go try at the hospital in Port Elizabeth.

MANNETJIE: But they said on the wireless . . .

ALFRED: I know. I was mos sitting here with you when we heard it. But that's the way it is with the government. Talk, talk, talk. Big promises . . . and then nothing happens. How is she?

MANNETJIE: Doesn't want to eat.

ALFRED: Leave the food here on the table. I'll try later when she wakes up. You can go play now if you want to. I'll watch her.

(Alfred goes to the bed and looks down at the sleeping Veronica. Mannetjie remains at the table.)

Doesn't look so good, hey. *(Shaking his head)* Not right, is it. She's such a special person, so clever and then all her songs . . . but look now. There she lies. And so thin! Makes you think, doesn't it. We pray, we sing hymns on Sunday . . . but there she lies.

MANNETJIE *(Hissing desperately)*: Stop it!

ALFRED *(Innocently)*: Stop what?

MANNETJIE: Stop talking like that!

ALFRED: Like what?

MANNETJIE: Like . . . like she's . . . because she's not. She's going to get better.

ALFRED: I was just feeling sorry for her, Mannetjie. I wasn't wishing for anything bad to happen. I pray all the time to God for her to get better every Sunday in church and every night on my knees by my bed. I know she is your mommy but she is also my Veronica. And just like you love your mommy, I also got my own feelings for her. To see her lying there like that . . . hell, man, Mannetjie! . . . it hurts me. Ja! If you knew all the feelings I got inside me for her, you wouldn't be so cross with me all the time.

(Looking down at Veronica as the memories of her come back to him.)

I remember the day when she left us. She was always talking about going one day but I didn't believe her. I mean . . . Veronica gone? Nonsense! But suddenly one day there it was. She was crying and hugging and kissing Oupa goodbye. She was also crying a little while I carried her suitcase to Mr. Vyver's old bakkie. I put it in the back, she waved good-bye to me, climbed in next to the old man, and off they went. And then . . . I don't know . . . empty. Nothing. I haven't got the words to tell you what it was like as I stood there and watched the dust and listened to the rattles of the old bakkie get softer and softer . . . until . . . nothing.

It was like she took away something more than just her clothes in the suitcase. Everything was empty, Mannetjie. Ja. That's it. That's what it felt like. Inside me and outside as well. She has made everything, the whole valley . . . empty! Haai! Those were sad days. Because that is when the other boys started teasing me again. "Where's your wife, Witbooi? She divorce you?" *(Wry little laugh)* But life is strange, Mannetjie! Because look now—she's my wife and I am also her husband. And because of that, now I also got you. *(Back at the table. Dismissively . . .)* Ag! . . . Don't listen to me. I talk too much. I must go just now. I didn't cook my supper yet. *(Lifts the lid off the pot on the table and examines its contents)* You made it?

MANNETJIE: Yes.

ALFRED: Smells good.

(After a few moments of hesitation, Mannetjie fetches a bowl and spoon and gives Alfred some of the soup.)

Keep some for yourself and your mommy. I just want a little bit. *(Points to the open book on the table)* Homework?

MANNETJIE: No. Just reading for Mommy.
ALFRED: What's the book?

(Mannetjie holds up the book so that Alfred can see the cover.)

It's the one you got in the reading competition in Graaff-Reinet, hey.
MANNETJIE: Yes.
ALFRED: I like the picture. *(Trying hard to engage Mannetjie)* Ja . . . first prize! Remember how excited and happy that made her? You would think she was the one who got the first prize.

(Pause. Mannetjie pages idly through the book. Alfred tries again.)

So what is happening in school?
MANNETJIE: Nothing.
ALFRED: Learning something new?
MANNETJIE: No. We're getting ready for the exams now.
ALFRED: You'll do good. I didn't. Your mommy tried hard to help me. *(Whispering)* She use to cheat for me. Write down the answers on my hand. But one time the teacher saw it and sent me to the principal. He made me bend down and then six times on the bum with a thin little quince stick. Those are the ones that hurt most. You try sitting down after that! I'd rather take a slap in the face any day to one of those.

(He laughs. Mannetjie doesn't.)

You never got it like that, hey.
MANNETJIE: No.
ALFRED: Because you're clever. Like your ma. You will come first again in the exams, won't you?
MANNETJIE: Yes.

ALFRED: Good! And then in two years' time: the big school in Graaff-Reinet!

(*Mannetjie shakes his head.*)

Hey . . . don't be like that! That's what your ma wants. It will make her so sad if . . .

MANNETJIE (*Interrupting Alfred angrily*): Don't be stupid, man. I know what my ma wants, but we haven't got the money for it.

ALFRED: But it's a free school, remember? I asked and they said it was free. Even the books.

MANNETJIE: It's the other things, man! The school uniform, accommodation . . .

(*Alfred doesn't know what "accommodation" means.*)

. . . a place to stay! Mommy is too sick now to go and ask for help like she was wanting to do. And you can't do that.

ALFRED: I can try. You and your ma must just tell me what to say.

MANNETJIE: You don't know how to speak properly. You can't even read anymore, because you never knew how to do it. So just leave it alone. You can't help me.

(*Alfred has taken the insults without flinching or anger. He knows that they are mostly true. After a long pause, he speaks softly:*)

ALFRED: Yes, I can.
MANNETJIE: What?
ALFRED: Help you.
MANNETJIE (*Scornfully*): You help me?
ALFRED: Yes.
MANNETJIE: How?

(Pause.)

ALFRED: I got money.

MANNETJIE *(Scornfully)*: How much? Ten rand?

ALFRED: More.

MANNETJIE: Twenty rand?

ALFRED: Much more than twenty rand, Mannetjie. Much, much more than twenty rand.

(Something in Alfred's tone silences Mannetjie. The two of them stare at each other wordlessly for a few seconds, at the end of which Alfred obviously makes a decision.)

Okay!

(He leaves the table and fetches his old canvas sling bag from the nail next to the door. He takes out two Horse Shoe tobacco bags and places then in front of Mannetjie.)

Go on. Open them.

(A bewildered Mannetjie does nothing. Alfred takes one of the bags, opens it and empties its contents on the table. Rand banknotes fall to the table.)

I can't count them. When the number gets too big I get frightened and then I get mixed-up and I got to start again. You count them. I know you will get it right. And then we can see how much it is.

MANNETJIE *(Appalled and suspicious)*: Where did you get it?

ALFRED: Shh . . . not so loud. Your ma might hear. It's all right, Mannetjie—I know God is going to punish me. I did tell him in church what I done. So there it is now.

MANNETJIE: But where did you get it? Did you steal it?

ALFRED (*Squirming*): Mannetjie . . . please, man. Don't be cross with me. It was the devil what made me take it. I never done it before in my life . . . but this time . . . because it was so much . . . you see . . . I never seen so much money before in my life . . . I didn't ever know Oupa was doing it . . . he never said anything to me all the time we was working together and anyway . . . he was already dead such a long time . . .

(Mannetjie is shaking his head with incomprehension. Alfred calms down.)

Okay. I'll tell you slowly. It was the time when your Oupa Buks was still alive—when him and me was working together on the akkers. You see, like I told you he was always talking about your mama. Veronica this and Veronica that, and how she used to sing for him, and how pretty she looked when she went to church. He was talking about your ma, Mannetjie. We didn't know yet about you because you wasn't born yet. Like I told you, the one thing he was always saying is that she would come back one day. He believed in that so much that he made me believe in it also. So when we was there on the akkers working and he would stop and say, "She is coming back, Alfred." I would also say, "Yes, Oupa Buks, she is coming back." But you see he was also getting old and more and more sick. Every time when there was something new wrong with him he would tell me to go to the clinic and tell Sister Wessels where it was hurting him and she would give me pills for him. Sometimes also medicine in a bottle to rub on the sore place. And because it was like that with him he started to worry about everything . . . 'specially this house, where we are sitting now. "If something happens to me, Alfred, you must look after it for Veronica," he said, because one day she is coming back.

He made me promise. "Promise me you will do that," he said. So I promised him. But you know, all the time I could see there was something else he wanted to tell me. So many time when we was working he would stop and say, "Alfred, listen to me now . . ." And I would say, "Yes, Oupa, I am listening." And then him, "There is something I must tell you." And then me, "What is it, Oupa?" And he would stand and think and look at me in a hard way, and then shake his head and say, "Never mind. It's nothing," and then go on working. Then he died. There on the akkers. Anyway, that is when I took all the things that was in here and kept it at my place. The next thing I know is that one day I get a big surprise. Because Oupa was now dead I didn't go to the post office anymore to see if there was a letter for him from you. But I'm walking along one day when Mrs. Claassen of the post office stops me in the street. "Alfred," she says, "when are you coming to fetch your two letters?" So I said to her, "Don't you know Oupa Buks is already dead?" And she says, "Only one letter is for him the other letter is for you." I thought she was just teasing me, but she wasn't. There it was, the letter from your mama for him and the other letter from your mommy for me, saying she was coming back and I must please get the place ready for her. Let me tell you now that that was quite a job, Mannetjie. The dust and the spiderwebs and the mouse kak was everywhere. So I'm working hard to make it clean when one day a big Red Roman spider comes in and starts running around on the floor. Mannetjie, I'm telling you that one would win the spider races any day! Anyway, he is running around in here and I'm trying to kill him with my broom when he shoots under the bed. I pull it away. I got the broom ready. I see him and I start hitting and that is when I see your oupa's hiding place. It's there . . . *(Points to the bed)* . . . under the bed, behind one of the bricks in the wall. Something didn't look right to me because I can see one of the bricks is loose. So I take it out and there it is, those two bags with the money. When I opened them, I couldn't believe what I was seeing. You must know, Mannetjie, I never seen so much money in all my life. And when I am looking and thinking, "Where did Oupa Buks get all this money?" I see that piece of white paper . . .

(He retrieves a paper slip from the pile of money.)

. . . And then I know what it is. Pension payment slip. Ja! Oupa was saving all his pension money. And now comes my big sin, why God is waiting to get his hands on me. When I am looking at the money I start to think there is enough to buy a bicycle, a brand-new red bicycle with a bell and a pump and a light . . . the bicycle Veronica made me dream about before she went to Cape Town. I also knew then that your Oupa was saving that money for her when she came back, but it didn't help, because I just couldn't stop seeing that red bicycle! So I took the money home with me and made another hiding place for it. I also said to myself, "It's not yours, Alfred. Give it to Veronica when she comes back just like Oupa would have done." Truly, Mannetjie. Every night I say that. But hey! . . . The devil is strong. He makes it that every night I can also see myself sitting on that bicycle and riding around the village ringing the bell and laughing and waving at all the people that use to laugh at me. So I didn't give it back.

MANNETJIE: You wanted to steal it?

ALFRED: Yes.

MANNETJIE: To buy that bicycle?

ALFRED: Yes.

MANNETJIE: My mama's money?

ALFRED: Yes.

MANNETJIE: Money to buy medicines and other things to make
her feel better?

ALFRED: Mannetjie, please listen to me. I . . .

*(The dammed-up emotions in the young boy can no longer be
contained. Their release comes in a violent physical assault on
Alfred, who makes no attempt to retaliate. The assault is all
the more vicious because it is accompanied by hissed whispers
. . . "I hate you . . . hate you . . . hate you." They build to
a climax, where they change into sobbing as he collapses onto
Alfred's chest. After a few tentative seconds, Alfred enfolds the
distraught Mannetjie in his arms. He speaks gently:)*

No! No! Stop now. It's all right. You did right to punish
me, Mannetjie. God is also going to do that. Because I will
also tell him everything. But I will also tell him and you
that the money is here on the table because I was going to
give it back to you and your mommy tonight. When I was
talking to your mommy about her sickness, she told me
the medicines to make her better was costing thousands
and thousands of rands. Every month. There is a lot of
money, but Oupa couldn't have saved that much. There
isn't that much there.

(Points to the money on the table) It has been so hard for
me to keep that money and dream about the red bicycle.
When I was working on the akkers this morning, getting
it ready for the pumpkin seeds, it was like I could see your
oupa sitting there under the walnut tree where he died.
He was looking at me and I felt so ashamed, Mannetjie!
When I was finished working, I went to my house, took
the money from its hiding place, put it in my bag and
came here.

I know I should have done it a long time ago, but it is
not altogether too late. It can still do some good. Because
you know how much your mama wants you to go to the

big school and go on learning. The money will help us
do that.

*(Pause. Mannetjie calms down slowly and disengages himself
from Alfred's arms.)*

Okay. So there it is. I will go now.

*(He goes to the door, collects his bag and then turns for a last
word to Mannetjie.)*

When your mama wakes up, you must tell her everything
I told you. And please . . . don't forget to tell her how
sorry I am for what I did. *(Turns to leave)*
MANNETJIE *(Impulsively)*: No . . . don't!

(Pause. Alfred waits at the door.)

ALFRED: What?
MANNETJIE: Don't go.
ALFRED: Why? What's wrong?

(Mannetjie looks at the bed and his sleeping mother.)

MANNETJIE: I'm frightened.

*(Alfred also looks at the sleeping Veronica and knows what Man-
netjie means.)*

ALFRED: Ja . . . me also. Sometimes when I think about it, about
what's going to happen, I don't even want to come here
anymore. It wasn't like that with my sick mother but, you
see, I didn't have deep feelings for her anymore. Sometimes I was even hoping it would happen very quick with
her because it was taking so long! But with Veronica . . .
oh my God, no!

(He looks at the little boy for a few seconds, makes a decision, and then joins him at the table.)

You know something, Mannetjie . . . I think we must be together for this one, face whatever is going to happen together. It's too much for one of us alone. But together, we can help each other . . . when the time comes. Make each other strong. What do you say?

(Pause. He and the young boy look into each other's eyes honestly and openly.)

It's what she wanted, you know.

MANNETJIE: Yes, I know.

ALFRED: Okay then?

MANNETJIE: Yes, okay.

(Alfred puts his bag back on the nail in the wall and returns to the table.)

ALFRED: You look very tired. I think you must go to bed now and sleep. And don't worry, I'll go sit with her and keep watch.

(Alfred goes and sits at Veronica's bedside. Mannetjie watches him.)

MANNETJIE: So . . . what do you want me to call you now? *(Repeating himself to get Alfred's attention)* What must I call you now?

ALFRED: What do you mean?

MANNETJIE: Do you want to be my "pa" or my "oom" . . . or what?

ALFRED: Ag no, Mannetjie. Forget about all that. Your ma was just trying everything she could think of to make it right between us. And now she has. Isn't that so? I want to be your friend and . . . you know my name.

MANNETJIE: So . . . just "Alfred."

ALFRED: That's me. Put that money away nicely and we'll give it to her when she wakes up. It's hers now. That's who Oupa Buks was saving it for.

(Alfred turns back to his bedside vigil.

Mannetjie, at the table, looks down at the pile of banknotes in front of him, then slowly collects them together and puts them back into the bag. Then he picks up the pumpkin seed tin and, holding it with both hands, tries to conjure up an image of the old man.

The scene segues slowly into Oupa's entrance. He is in a buoyant, upbeat mood and laughing quietly to himself as he places his spade against the wall next to the door. He brings with him into the room the sound of the Cape turtledove.)

OUPA *(Joining Mannetjie at the table)*: Ja! Listen! Do you hear them?

MANNETJIE: Yes.

OUPA: Do you know what they are saying?

MANNETJIE: No.

OUPA: "Work HARder—work HARder—work HARder" . . . Every blue gum tree in the village has got its tortelduifie telling us: to "work HARder, work HARder." Ja! It's that time of the year again. I see you got your seeds ready. So what you waiting for? Grab your spade and go to the akkers. The wind pump is throwing up water, the sun is shining. I'm telling you now: it's going to be a good year. I can feel it. You just wait and see if I am not right. When you stuff your mouth full of juicy, sweet Hanepoot korrels, or when you put a big, flat white Boer pumpkin on the roof, remember what I said to you. When you pick ertjies, pull out carrots and dig potatoes . . . remember what I said tonight and thank the Lord when you kneel at your bed. You saw what happens when he is cross with us . . .

that late frost that killed everything. Were you here that winter? I forget now what year it was. Believe me, you were lucky if you weren't. It was the worst one I have lived through in all my years . . . and I don't know how many years is that—I stopped counting a long, long time ago. Ja, that winter? But God is good. One night I'm lying in here again, slowly going into the darkness, when I hear it: "Work harder! . . . Work harder . . . Work harder! . . ." A tortelduifie sitting somewhere in a bloekomboom telling us all that it is spring. A few days later Alfred and I were on the akkers once again planting pumpkin seeds. It was such a big feeling. I knew that I was going to taste Hanepoot grapes one more time, pick ertjies and tomatoes, and put a big, flat white pumpkin on the roof in February. Do you know what it is like to be planting again in warm sunshine with tortelduifies in all the trees helping you to work harder! Ha! That is happiness, my friend. Real happiness. And then do you know what it is like a few days later to see the first green little fingers pushing though the soil so that they can also drink sunshine? Watch the first little leaves open? That is when you stand in church on Sunday and try to sing louder then anybody else because you want to thank the Lord. And then my friend, do you know what it is like another few days later when you lie in your bed at night and feel the cold come back? Because that time it did. And I knew while I was lying there, trying to keep warm again, I knew that the late frost had come into the valley to burn all the small pumpkin plants black. Ja! I was right. When I went to the akkers next morning, there they were . . . black . . . dead . . . all of them. Black and dead. Alfred was standing there with me. "Why, Oupa?" he asked. "Why must the frost come now? We worked so hard." I shook my head, and I think I made a little noise, because he looked at me and asked if I was all right. I said, "Ja, I'm all right. It's nothing. Just nothing. Dig them up, Alfred," I said, "and plant again." Then I walked over to the walnut tree to rest—my legs was feeling very tired. Because, you see, it wasn't nothing. When Alfred asked, "Why, why must the frost come now just when the little pumpkin plants are starting to grow?" I remembered another time when it was just like that. I was still only a little boy and I was standing with my pa and we were also looking at little plants that had been burnt black by the frost—ertjies and tomatoes that time, we hadn't planted our pumpkins yet—and it was me who asked, "Why? We worked so hard, Pa," I said. "Why must it come now?" "It was a late frost," my father said. "I know, Pa," I said, "but why now?" "Because that's the way it is," he said. "But why is it that way just when the little seeds are starting to grow?" "Because that is the way it is with the late frost." "But, Pa," I said, because I still had questions . . .

And that is when he hit me: "Listen now, Abraam"— nobody was yet calling me Buks—"Listen, Abraam," he said, "the why is because it is the late frost. You don't need to ask, 'Why?' Throw that word away. It's useless. 'Why' is because it is. Do you ask why the sun shines, the winds blows, the rain falls, the late frost comes? There is no 'why' to what God does. He is why. Finish and klaar."

And so it was that morning with me and Alfred. But I didn't hit him, I just made a little noise and walked to the walnut tree. It was like that late frost had also burnt black everything inside me. I was so tired as I sat down in the shade. The last thing I remember was Alfred's voice . . . far away . . . it was like he was very . . . very . . . far away . . . And he was calling me and laughing and saying that one little pumpkin plant was still alive . . . He was very surprised because it was green . . . it was still green and growing . . . Can you believe that? All the others dead or dying, but that little one still alive and growing . . .

(Oupa and Mannetjie study each other for a few seconds. Mannetjie is still holding his tin.)

So . . . What sort of seeds you got in your tin? Pumpkins? Carrots?

MANNETJIE: No.

(Pause.)

I got words.

OUPA: "Words"? What do you mean "words"?

MANNETJIE: Like the words we speak, Oupa. The words we write.

(Holding up the tin.)

These are my special words.

OUPA: But those aren't seeds.

MANNETJIE: They are *my* seeds.

OUPA *(A little chuckle of disbelief)*: So you are going to plant words?

MANNETJIE: Yes . . . they are also miracles. They will also grow.

OUPA *(Mystified)*: Where are you going to plant them?

MANNETJIE: In my akker.

OUPA *(Disbelief)*: You haven't got an akker!

MANNETJIE: I've got a place to plant them. Isn't that an akker?

OUPA *(Reluctantly)*: Yes, that is an akker.

(Mannetjie opens his exercise book, then his tin. He takes out his list of words.)

MANNETJIE: Watch now.

(He studies his list of words for a few seconds, then makes a choice. He picks up his pencil and starts writing in his exercise book.)

"Oupa's . . . Fan . . . tas . . . tic . . . Mir . . . acle.

"In a bygone age there was an old man called Oupa. He had a small tin full of pumpkin seeds . . . "

(Oupa nods his head, listening while Mannetjie writes.)

END OF PLAY

Have You Seen Us?

For Gordon Edelstein

PRODUCTION HISTORY

Have You Seen Us? received its world premiere at the Long
Wharf Theatre (Gordon Edelstein, Artistic Director; Ray
Cullom, Managing Director) in New Haven, Connecticut,
on December 2, 2009. The production was directed by Gordon Edelstein; the set designer was Eugene Lee, the costume
designer was Jennifer Von Mayrhauser, the lighting designer
was Stephen Strawbridge, the sound designer was Corrine K.
Livingston, the dramaturg was Anne Erbe, the stage manager
was Jason Kaiser. The cast was:

HENRY PARSONS	Sam Waterston
ADELA	Liza Colón-Zayas
SOLLY	Sol Frieder
RACHEL	Elaine Kussack

CHARACTERS

HENRY PARSONS: expatriate South African. University lecturer in medieval English literature. Divorced. Alcoholic. A weak and lonely man. Early sixties.

ADELA VENEGAS: Hispanic. Overweight. Essentially vulnerable and insecure but tries her best to hide it behind a front of aggressive superiority. Thirties.

SOLLY AND RACHEL: an elderly married couple. They both look and sound like Eastern European Jews.

Prologue

The sidewalk of a small shopping mall in Southern California. Christmas lights decorate the surrounding houses. It is night. Henry walks into the tent of golden light thrown down by a street light.

He has a book under his arm.

He hears the music to "Rudolph the Red-Nosed Reindeer" and begins to hum, whistle or sing along with it.

He talks directly to the audience:

HENRY: Have you ever wondered about those simple little accidents, those seemingly insignificant coincidences that go on to have a major effect on your life? Sometimes it is just a fleeting and apparently inconsequential encounter with a stranger, but like that first domino standing on end in the carefully assembled stack . . . when it goes down, one by one all the others go down with it. After all, that's the way it happens to us . . . Not so? We carefully line up all our dominoes . . . until that fateful little finger comes along and lightly touches the first one. It's happened to me a couple of times. The most recent and probably the most important was Christmas Eve two years ago, when I was standing on this very spot.

(He silently remembers that night, his failed marriage, the birth of his child and his dismissal from his academic job—all candidates for touching off the falling line of dominoes.
He looks around.)

Not a very glamorous one for a life-changer is it . . . a struggling little mall in Southern California? *(Pointing as he lists the shops in the mall)* There's a large parking lot in front of me and ringed around it is a supermarket . . . hairdresser . . . martial arts . . . Sizzling Chicken . . . that's behind me—it closed about half an hour ago—Family Dental Care . . . Mobile U cell phones . . . drugstore . . . and way down there, tucked away inconspicuously in a corner, there used to be a little sandwich shop.

A few attempts at jollification are around because it's that time of the year again . . . The supermarket has put up the same Christmas tree and strings of fancy lights it's had for the past few years, but the drugstore has tried something new this time . . . a big white-lights reindeer leaping off into space pulling Father Christmas in a sleigh loaded with presents. What made it all even more sad on that Christmas Eve two years ago is that it was raining. Yes! . . . The reflection of all those fancy lights had been turned into a wonderful display of multicolored smudges on the shiny wet tarmac surface of the lot. Not that I was in a mood to admire anything that night. Oh no. My mood was very . . . very different. Come to think of it, if I had sunk any deeper into the bog of self-pitying misery I was floundering around in, I might even have missed that touch of Fate's little finger altogether. You see, my visit to the sandwich shop for my usual order of turkey on whole wheat with sprouts and tomato and a cup of coffee had once again ended up with the waitress—Adela—winning the ugly little game that we used to play when we were alone in the shop, which was very often the case, of trading insults and offensive jibes with each other. Stupid, wasn't it? Two adult human beings behaving like that . . . and on Christmas Eve! But that's how it was. With half of my sandwich uneaten, I just grabbed my book and left.

(Pretend and pompous outrage) An overweight, uneducated Mexican waitress had once again humiliated me, Henry Parsons, PhD!

(A little laugh at himself.)

That was the game, you see—who could do it most effectively to the other. Because, make no mistake about it, we genuinely despised each other. That's right. I know she saw me for what I was. In fact, her winning volley that Christmas Eve was to tell me that she had seen me for a "borracho perdido" the very first time I walked in. Do you know what that means? "Worthless, lost, useless drunk"! On my side, I most certainly saw that tub of Mexican grease for what she was. So why was I in that crummy little sandwich shop? You tell me. Addicted to humiliation, maybe? Most likely. I know something about addiction . . . being one of Bill's friends. But to get back to that Christmas night, a month ago, when I ended up here. This very spot. And that is why I was back here last year and that is why I am back here again tonight. And I'll be back here again next year . . . God willing! It's the only anniversary in my life that means anything to me now. You see, I don't want to let go of what happened to me that night.

(A pause. Then he speaks carefully:)

I don't know how long I had been standing here, staring at nothing, when they, an old man and a woman, came shuffling past. It even took me a few seconds to register their greeting because when I looked up they were on the point of disappearing into the darkness. It was a simple greeting from a foreign sounding voice: "Good night, mister!" I managed to get out a polite response: "And a good night to the two of you!" . . . and then added: ". . . and a happy Christmas."

The two figures stopped and one of them turned to me—I couldn't see his face but I heard him clearly enough: "Thank you, sir, but we are Jews."

He waited for a few seconds and turned away and then, taking the woman by the hand, led her off slowly into the darkness. All sounds innocent enough, doesn't it?

(A little rueful shake of the head. He continues with calm detachment:)

I suppose it's because of what Adela had done to me that I reacted the way I did. I didn't say anything, but I was seething with resentment and hurt inside as I watched them fade away into the darkness. I know now that it wasn't meant that way, but at that moment it felt like another rejection and that was just once too often in my life. Thank God, that wasn't the end of it. That was the fateful touch all right, but my dominoes only started going down a couple of months later in the sandwich shop. Yes, I know what you're thinking! "You mean you went back there?" Yes, I did. In all fairness to myself, though, after that night I tried very hard to break the addiction, I stopped coming to this mall altogether. There is a much bigger one further along the highway. And I moved in there, trying out everything from frosted and jam-filled Dunkin' Donuts that made me nauseous to a Polo Loco pita pouch stuffed with beans and chilies and beef strips that gave me terrible indigestion that night . . . I won't go into the burger at Wendy's or what they tried to make me eat at Take-Away Tacos . . . Suffice it to say that I ended up wandering around that mall like a hungry canyon coyote sniffing up the garbage bins in the hope of finding something edible—and please know that tormenting me all the time was a vision of a simple, wholesome turkey sandwich on whole wheat with lettuce, tomato and sprouts. But what really made that holy grail of a sandwich totally irresistible was the thought that I could possibly spice it with a dash of *revenge*! Oh yes . . . I wasn't going to let that ill-mannered Mexican trollop get the better of me. When I had worked out how I was going to do that, I braced myself and came back to the sandwich shop. What I'd decided was that I would start out being polite . . . civilized . . . totally unarmed . . . and then when she was completed confused . . . *(Viciously—with an appropriate gesture aimed at Adela's solar plexus)* . . . give it to her.

I brooded on it for a few weeks and when I had worked out how I was going to get it, I braced myself and came back to the sandwich shop. I'd start out polite, keeping quiet, but then, when she was totally confused by my approach, I would let her have it. When I entered it she was behind the counter with her back turned to the door, and she was quietly singing along with a catchy little tune coming out of a small radio on the counter. I had never heard her singing before, so that was a surprise enough to start with. But what really stopped me dead in my tracks in the doorway was her voice. She was singing too softly for me to really hear it, but just occasionally she lifted it and then I caught a hint of a beautiful, rich, deep contralto. It reminded me of a voice I already knew. I was still trying to place it (Janet Baker? No. Christa Ludwig? No.) when she turned around and saw me. She immediately stopped singing and to hide her acute embarrassment launched an immediate attack—she greeted me with a laugh and a, "Welcome back, my borracho perdido."

(*Gloating*) But I had done my homework . . . this time I was ready for her.

The Sandwich Shop

A few tables and chairs, a counter and a chalkboard menu. Adela is behind the counter singing softly, as Henry described in the Prologue.

Henry walks in, takes off his raincoat. He is dressed shabbily, his clothes unlaundered. He pauses in the doorway, listening to Adela. She turns around and sees him, and immediately stops singing. She switches off the radio and starts making his usual sandwich, at the same time doing her best to hide her confusion and embarrassment. Henry strolls nonchalantly to a table, feigning total indifference to her presence.

ADELA *(Aggressively, as she makes his sandwich)*: Welcome back, my dear old borracho perdido. Sucio viejo borracho. You know that one, darling? I teach you. Yes, I like you so much you sucio viejo borracho perdido, I teach you speak my language. "Sucio" is meaning "dirty." "Viejo" is "old." Sí. There you have it. And who is sucio viejo borracho perdido? My sucio viejo borracho perdido . . . is you!

(She thinks this is very funny. Henry is putting on a very good performance of not having heard a word of what she said as he opens his book, places his bookmark on the table and starts to read. The sandwich is now finished and Adela brings it to the table.)

HENRY: What is this, señorita?

ADELA: You also blind now? Is your sandwich.

HENRY: But I haven't ordered anything yet.

ADELA: Turkey on whole wheat . . .

HENRY: That is not what I want today.

ADELA *(Getting flustered and angry)*: Is your sandwich, I tell you. You order every time.

HENRY: My dear señorita —I say "señorita" incidentally because I think anyone would have to be blind, dead and dumb to want to marry you—so I say, señorita, it is not what I want so take the fucking thing back and wait for my order!

ADELA: You eat it or go!

HENRY: No.

*(Pause.
    Adela stares back at him with impotent fury.)*

That's right . . . NO! So go ahead and call the police if you want to. But before you do so let me just say I hope your papers are in order, darling, because that is the first thing they are going to ask for, you know. I've got no problem and I certainly hope for your sake that you haven't any as well. Know what I mean? Like you being ilegalidad . . . you know, illegal immigrante? . . . which if you want a lesson in your own language means they will arrest you, lock you up and then kick your fat Mexican arse all the way back to Tijuana.

ADELA *(Slowly picks up the sandwich she had placed in front of Henry)*: So what you want?

HENRY: That's better! Now let's see . . .

(Exploiting his command of the situation, he studies the menu.)

You know something, Tubby . . . I think we'll sample your roast beef on rye . . . Yes . . . that should be nice . . . Make it roast beef on rye with sweet deli mustard, sprouts and a few slices of tomato. And while you're about it, put a few jalapeño peppers on the side. And then, of course, my usual cup of coffee.

(A still, silent Adela glares at him for a few seconds before going back to the counter and dumping the turkey sandwich in the trash. Henry is putting up a great show; humming unconcernedly as he starts to read. Adela turns on the radio to full volume. Very loud Mexican music and static come from it. Henry looks up from his book.)

Could you turn down the volume a little please? I am trying to read, you know.

(Adela waits, then turns down the volume.)

Don't get me wrong; I like the music—that song you were singing when I came in was quite lovely—it's the atmospherics I can't stand, you know, all that crackling and spitting like bacon in a frying pan.

(A little laugh at his image of bacon in a frying pan.
He tries to hum the song she was singing when he arrived.)

Hum-de-dum-dum da-da-da . . . is that how it went? Your little song?

(Still no response from Adela. The sandwich is finished. She brings it to the table with a cup of coffee. Henry is again full of bland smiles for her as she puts his sandwich and coffee down on

the table. She is standing there looking for an opening when she sees the bookmark—it is a letter-sized mailing card. She picks it up and studies it.)

ADELA: What is this?

HENRY *(Hoping to catch her)*: Read it . . . or do we add illiteracy to your many other disqualifications?

ADELA *(Accepting the challenge, reading carefully)*: "Have You Seen Us?" So . . . missing peoples.

HENRY: "Missing persons" is the correct expression. They come in the mail. About one a week. I've got a stack of one eighty-seven of them on my desk. I use them as bookmarks. This is number eighty-eight—Isabella and Adriana Larranaga.

(Adela pounces. With a snort of derision, she gives him the correct pronunciation of the name.)

ADELA: Larrañaga . . . ñaga . . . ñaga . . . ñaga . . . Larrañaga.

HENRY *(Returning her volley with a smile)*: Of course . . . and thank you, Tubby. Larrañaga.

ADELA: You with your books . . . you think you know so much! You may be teacher but you know nothing! You must learn to speak Spanish! So I teach you. *(Studying the card and nodding knowingly)* Mother and daughter.

HENRY: Maybe. Little Isabella is the missing person, Adriana is the last person she was seen with. There's a good probability, of course, that they are mother and—

ADELA *(Cutting him short)*: There's no probable and there's no maybe. Look, man. You blind? Look eyes and mouth. *(Tapping the two small pictures on the card)* Same . . . same! Mama Adriana and her pretty daughter, little Isabella. I know why they missing. I know their story.

HENRY: And I don't want to hear it!

(In a pretense of being bored with what she is saying, Henry gives a heavy sigh and shake of his head, then starts to eat his sandwich and drink his coffee.)

ADELA: I'm telling it. So you listen and learn, gringo. Husband is beating wife, Adriana. Right? Wife calls police and wants divorce. Okay? Next stop: court case. Police and husband tell lies in court but judge believes him because they all gringos and husband is Vietnam vet. Verdict? Court gives baby Isabella to husband. They call it American justice. But not end of story because now comes Mexican justice. Beautiful Adriana waits for time when little Isabella is playing in the street. Adriana walks—very easy, like you know—to Isabella and says . . . "Hey baby! Come with Mama! We go eat ice cream." . . . And off they go.

(A triumphant little laugh ends her narrative.)

And there you have it. Now Daddy is loading his Vietnam gun and looking for them.

(She hands back the card with another snort of derision.)

So you think they gonna walk in here and order two bowls of chili and then you make phone call and get reward? Well. You can forget it, and you wanna know why?

HENRY: No.

ADELA: Because Isabella and Adriana is now in Mexico. With the grandmother. Yes. Look at her! She not a fool. That woman got brains. Husband maybe got the gun but she's got the brains and there no maybes or probables in that head. You think she gonna go sit in McDonald's and eat hamburgers waiting for him to find them and then shoot up the whole fucking place and kill fifteen people? No way. She and girlie safe and singing "Down Mexico Way." Like I tell you, is a good American story.

HENRY: Groundless speculation, my dear . . . and if you don't mind me saying so . . . very uninteresting. Now stop wasting my time and get back behind the counter . . .

ADELA (*Once again cutting him short*): You don't like it? Too bad. But that's the way it is. Sí. And you wanna know why? You a man, husband a man, judge a man . . . and all of you gringos. Poor Adriana is just Mexican, so who cares? Not you. Not nobody.

(*Shaking her head, she takes the card back and speaks directly to the picture of Adriana*) Don't come back here, baby, because you had it in America!

(*She hands the photo back to Henry. With a little laugh she sails back triumphantly to the counter.*)

HENRY: Just for the record . . . I am not an American.

ADELA: You still gringo . . . and me? . . . (*With pride*) . . . Mexican!

(*Her proud boast makes Henry pause and think.*)

HENRY: Well played! I'll give you that point. I can't trump your pride . . . and for the simple reason that I don't think I've got any left. (*He tries*) "I am a South African!" Didn't sound convincing, did it? Certainly didn't feel it. But there was a time . . . oh yes, there was a time . . .

(*He shakes his head ruefully.*
Pause.
He starts eating his sandwich and waits, watching her at work behind the counter for a minute or so, beginning to see her as something more than just a target for his scorn and contempt. Eventually . . .)

Do you ever get homesick?

ADELA: Homesick? Home? Sick?

(It takes her a few seconds to realize what the word means.)

Ah . . . nostalgico . . . morriña . . . *(Suddenly suspicious)* Why you asking? You report me to Immigration?

HENRY: No . . . no . . . no! God, no! Forget it. *(Goes back to his coffee)* We had enough of that back home in the old days. Please . . . I was just asking because I use to get it.

ADELA: So . . . nostalgico? Sí . . . Many times. For my village . . . Estancio de los Lopez . . . I get very sick for the time when my abuelita was alive . . . my . . . what you call it? . . . my grandma. My mama die when I was still baby, so Grandma she look after me. My father, he leave us with other men in the village to come to America and look for job, but we don't hear from him again. Some people think they all die in the desert. Now I only got my hermano . . . my brother . . . Ignacio . . . Sometimes he speaks to me on the telephone and that makes me get bad nostalgico.

HENRY: I used to get it bad, too. Hardly ever nowadays but when I first came to America! . . . It actually made me cry a couple of times . . . when I was alone. Walking around New York talking to myself like a madman . . . in Afrikaans . . . my mother's language . . . singing silly little songs because I was frightened that I would forget how to speak it.

ADELA: You sing songs?

HENRY: From my alma mater, the Stellenbosch University rugby song. *(With a laugh he launches into an Afrikaans folksong:)*

Bobbejaan klim die berg
So haastig en so lastig.
Bobbejaan klim die berg
So haastig en so lastig.
Bobbejaan klim die berg.
Om die boere te vererg.
Hoera vir die jollie bobbejaan.

O moenie huil nie,
O moenie treur nie,
Die Stellenbosse boys kom weer.

(Baboon climbs the mountain
So quickly while he teases. (x2)
Baboon climbs the mountain,
Teasing farmers when he pleases.
Hooray for our jolly baboon.

But please don't cry, dear,
Don't ever sigh, dear,
The Stellenbosch boys will soon be back.)

(Adela thinks his performance hilariously funny.)

Oh God! It's all there, isn't it? How can a silly little song
like that capture so much? . . . I can still see that koppie—
that's the Afrikaans word for mountain. I've scrambled to
the top of a hundred of them . . . sat down on a warm,
sun-baked red sandstone boulder . . . barked back at the
baboons, watched black eagles tumbling around in a blue
sky . . . and then, there in New York, the dreams about it
at night . . . wake up with such a yearning in my heart . . .
lying there in bed I think I would have traded my soul to
be standing on a street corner anywhere in South Africa
for just one day . . . that was another terrible yearning . . .
watching people live their lives . . . and understanding what
those lives were all about. I can't do that here in America.
I understand nothing. When I stand on a street corner
here in America I feel I don't even speak the same language. Back there it was different . . . I knew them all . . .
I knew their stories . . . the little barefoot boys in khaki
shorts, the tired black mothers and grandmothers with a
few precious groceries in a plastic bag, the out-of-work

fathers! . . . That sounds like a homesick South African doesn't it. But that was all a long time ago.

ADELA *(Having been listening and watching him carefully)*: No. You still sick with it, gringo.

HENRY: With . . . what did you call it . . . nostalgico? Me? Now?

ADELA: Sí nostalgico . . . morriña. Still strong with you. I see it. In you. You . . .

(Adela is on the point of saying something more but he suddenly gestures that she must be silent. He then points excitedly at the little radio and speaks through a mouthful of his sandwich.)

HENRY: There! There it is again. That song. The one you were singing. Turn it up! Tubby! Turn it up!

(She finally realizes what he wants and turns up the volume.)

Come on! Sing! Please . . .

ADELA *(Shaking her head)*: No.

HENRY: Well, to hell with you then! If you won't, I will . . .
(Singing along with the tune from the radio) La la la la . . . da da dum . . . la la la la . . .

ADELA: Stop! Is terrible . . . terrible . . .

(She switches off the radio.)

Is my song!

HENRY: Your song? Since when is it "your song."

ADELA: Yes . . . is my song.

HENRY: What do you mean?

ADELA: Is my name song. "Adelita." That is song's name. My name is Adela . . . baby name is Adelita.

HENRY: Adelita . . . Adela . . . beautiful names . . . which incidentally you don't deserve! I could think of some more appropriate ones for you but let's forget that for the moment and just sing that bloody song for me. We can go on hating each other after that.

ADELA: No.

HENRY: Why not? I'm a customer and the customer is always right.

ADELA: You go to hell now. I not singing for you.

HENRY: Good heavens! I don't believe it . . . you won't sing because you are shy! *(A good laugh)* Listen, Tubby . . . you've got plenty of very good reasons for being shy, but your voice is, amazingly, not one them. God Almighty, but you really are stupid! It hurts me deeply to credit you with anything good but the truth is you *have* got a beautiful voice. Yes! No? Well, then teach me the words so that I can sing it.

ADELA: No . . . no! You mustn't. It is my song.

HENRY: Then sing it! Oh, for God's sake . . . what's the matter with you? Surely you've got enough intelligence to know that you *have* got a good voice. Somebody must have told you that.

(A pause. After staring at Henry for a few seconds, she turns her back to him and sings a few verses of "Adelita," sotto voce.
When she is finished, she tries to busy herself with counter work, her back still turned to him.)

(With simple sincerity) Thank you. Thank you very much. That was very beautiful . . . and leaves me amazed once again at the Almighty's infinite capacity for the really big mistake: that voice in your body. By the way, it reminds me of one of my favorite singers, Kathleen Ferrier. In her case the voice and the body were very appropriately matched. But there again, you see . . . just as she is reaching her glorious maturity, He goes along and plants a few cancer cells in her throat.

(Adela stops working behind the counter.)

Anyway . . . thank you . . . Adela.

(Henry goes back to his sandwich and coffee.
Continuing her work, her back still turned, Adela starts singing again—this time with a lot more volume. Halfway through the song, she turns around and faces Henry across the counter. He is listening with quiet appreciation. Silent hand clapping from Henry when she reaches the end.)

(With mock gravity) This is very bad! At this rate you are once again going to take the honors tonight. I haven't got anything in my arsenal to equal that.

(Embarrassed little gesture from Adela, but she is obviously very pleased with Henry's response to her singing. The possibility of a new relationship between the two of them is slowly becoming evident as the scene develops.)

What is the song about?
ADELA: I was telling you. Adelita. Song is about Adelita.
HENRY: But what do the words say about her?

(Adela comes out from behind the counter, but maintains a distance between herself and Henry. She quotes the Spanish lyrics of the song and tries to translate them for Henry's benefit.)

ADELA:
 Popular entre la tropa era Adelita
 (All the soldiers . . . they like Adela very much)
 la mujer que el sargento idolatraba . . . idolatraba . . .
 (The sergeant he . . . idolatraba . . .)

What is idolatraba?

HENRY: Idolize maybe . . . the sergeant idolizes her . . . the sergeant *loves* her?

ADELA: Sí . . . the sergeant, he loves her . . . and she loves him. She goes everywhere he goes . . . in the train, in the boat . . . everywhere. That is the way it was with the Soldaderas.

HENRY: Sol . . . dar . . . der . . .

ADELA: You don't know Soldaderas? You don't know Margarita Neri?

HENRY: No.

ADELA *(Shaking her head disapprovingly)*: Hey, gringo! You don't speak Spanish! You don't know *Soldaderas!* You don't know nothing, Mr. Professor. I tell you. Soldaderas is soldiers. *Woman soldiers.* Margarita Neri is most famous Soldadera. Sí. Soldaderas they fight in the Revolucion with the men soldiers. Sí! My grandmama was Soldadera. Dolores Galindo! Margarita Neri teach her how to shoot . . . you know . . . Bang! Bang! Sí. When I was little girl she tell me stories about Zapata. Emiliano Zapata. You don't know him also?

HENRY: No . . . I do know about him . . . that is, Hollywood's version of him, thanks to Marlon Brando. *Viva Zapata!* According to that film he was a good and a very brave man in the revolution. Right?

ADELA: ¡¡¡Sí!!! He is big hero for Mexican peoples. One time in the Revolucion my grandma she cook tortillas for him. She was telling me he sing "Adelita" with his camaradas. I got picture of her on the wall in my room when she was Soldadera with big revolver and long fusil for shooting far and bandalera with real bullets. But she is dead now.

HENRY: You miss her, don't you, Adela.

ADELA: ¡Sí! I miss her very much . . . very, very mucha. She is teaching me to sing "Adelita." Lots of other songs also . . . you know them? "Cielito Lindo"? Very famous song!

(She sings a snatch of the song:)

De la Sierra Morena,
Cielito lindo, vienen bajando,
Un par de ojitos negros,
Cielito lindo, de contrabando.

Estribillo:
Ay, ay, ay, ay,
Canta y no llores,
Porque cantando se alegran,
Cielito lindo, los corazones.

(From the brown mountain range,
Beautiful sky, they are coming down,
A pair of black eyes,
Beautiful sky, of contraband.

Sing and don't cry,
For singing gladdens the heart,
Heavenly one, the hearts.)

HENRY: Yes! I've heard that one.
ADELA: And "Besame Mucho"? *("Kiss Me, Kiss Me a Lot.")*

(She gives him a verse of that one as well.)

HENRY *(Delighted)*: You bet I do!
ADELA: She was very sick just before she dies so she always ask
   me to sit with her and sing. She also tell me I got good
   voice for singing. But when I sing always she cries. Even
   with the happy songs. "Grandma," I ask, "why you cry?"
   She just shake her head and tell me: "Go to America, my
   carino. Is no good in Mexico now. When you are big go to
   America." But I had to wait long time before I got enough
   money. My brother Ignacio, he also help me.
HENRY: How long have you been in America, Adela?

ADELA: Two years. *(Pause)* And you?

HENRY: Me? What?

ADELA: So tell me? Who are you?

HENRY *(Clearing his throat in mock preparation for a speech)*: My name is Henry Parsons. I am sixty-three years old and I've been in America for fifteen years. For a long time I tried to justify my existence by trying to arouse the interest of young minds in medieval literature . . . with particular emphasis, of course, on English . . . *Beowulf, Canterbury Tales, Charter of Cnut* and the like . . . anything in fact in Old English that nobody reads or speaks anymore. I am in other words a teacher of a dead language . . . and many has been the time when I though I was teaching it to the dead.

(Adela shakes her head uncomprehendingly.)

Sorry . . . I'm a teacher, Adela.

ADELA: In school?

HENRY: College. Young people.

ADELA: And you? You got family?

HENRY: I did have. They are now nine thousand nine hundred miles away. I'm divorced.

ADELA: For how long?

HENRY: Ten years.

ADELA: Children?

HENRY: One. A girl. Kate. A young woman now. But she was a little girl when I last saw her in person. She sends me photographs with her letters from time to time . . . but that only makes everything very much worse. You see, she was my best friend back in South Africa. She climbed with me to the top of many of those koppies where the baboons barked at us.

ADELA *(The missing persons card)*: Is it like Isabella and Adriana? You wife take little girl and go?

HENRY: Not quite. She did take little girl and go, but there was no fighting about it. As you can see, Adela, I am not loading my Vietnam gun and looking for them.

ADELA: So what happens?

HENRY *(Wearily)*: Oh God! Do you really want to know?

ADELA: Sí.

HENRY: All right, here's the story . . . the truth and nothing but the truth so help me God! I am, Adela, by common definition, an alcoholic: you were right, borracho perdido. Ten years ago my very beautiful wife—Loretta—delivered an ultimatum: "Me or the bottle."

ADELA *(Nodding her head in an "I knew it!" response)*: And you choose bottle. You got beautiful wife and little girl but you want bottle.

HENRY: No! It's not as simple as that! I wanted them. I wanted my family. So I tried! Believe me, I really tried. Every Saturday night in the basement room of a church in Gramercy Park in New York.

(He stands up as if in an AA meeting.)

"My name is Henry and I am an alcoholic."
"Welcome, Henry!"

(He sits down.)

ADELA: So how long this time?

HENRY: Without a drink?

ADELA: Sí.

HENRY: My last binge—a bottle of bourbon and enough maudlin tears to fill it up when it was empty—was last month, Christmas Eve. That's right. You remember? You had a hand in that little night of merriment. Proud of yourself? It was the night you made me feel so utterly worthless. Cried like a baby, I did in my apartment. Poor Henry!

ATHOL FUGARD

(Pause. Feeling his resentment and bile rising, he shakes his head.)

But for your information, Adela, I still try over here with
visits to another church basement . . . but it's a rather half-
hearted attempt now. You see, my daughter Kate has told
me that she would love to come and visit me, provided
I could stay sober for a year. So what do I do? I get to
ten, sometimes even eleven months . . . and then I hit the
bottle again. But I'm not fooling myself. I know what's
happening. Do I really want her to come over and look at
me, look at my what my life is now? Even if I was sober,
what would she see?

ADELA: Her papa is sad man.

HENRY: I think the word you want, Adela, is "pathetic."

ADELA: ¿Patetico? You?

HENRY: Yes . . . you know . . . miserable.

ADELA: Sí. Miserable.

HENRY: But you knew that very first day I walked in, didn't
you? Very obvious wasn't it? . . .

ADELA: That you drink too much? Sí. I watch you . . . you hand
shaking, you not shave, you stink . . . so I think: another
borracho perdido!

HENRY *(Sharply, a mixture of anger and fear)*: Hopeless! You are
saying I'm hopeless?

ADELA *(Defensively)*: Because mine was! Sí. I know borracho
perdido because I had him and he make a mess of Adela's
life. All the time promises, promises but nothing changes.
And then one day vamoose—last time I hear he is in Mexico City . . . eating dogshit in barrios bajos.

HENRY: So you kicked him out.

ADELA *(Ashamed)*: No . . . I was too much . . . you know . . . and
he make promises all the time.

HENRY: I understand. What was his name?

ADELA: Roberto.

HENRY: Children?

140

ADELA: No.

HENRY: I get it now. When I first walked in here last Christmas and you saw another borracho perdido . . . and you saw Roberto. Right?

ADELA *(Again defensively)*: Sí . . . because I no like borracho perdido.

HENRY: Relax, Adela. Nobody does.

(Pause. Both Adela and Henry take a deep breath. Both of them want to hold on to what was trying to happen between them.)

ADELA *(Timidly)*: So now . . . I don't know . . . maybe is different for you. *(Wagging a finger at him)* Maybe is better you go back to your wife now, Henry.

Yes. Because you also still got the nostalgico. I think maybe is easier for you there by your wife. Then you stop drinking.

HENRY: I should have done that a long time ago, Adela. It's too late now! My wife and daughter have made new lives for themselves and there is no place for me in them. In any case, my nostalgico is for a South Africa that doesn't exist anymore and the new one also hasn't got a place for me. Nobody there wants to learn what I want to teach . . . and that is all I can meaningfully do with my life. For the rest . . . I can't even hit a nail in straight.

ADELA *(Studying Henry with obvious sympathy)*: Okay. This is what you do. You sober now. Right?

HENRY: Yes . . . but I am not particularly enjoying it.

ADELA: Too bad. You do it . . . because you know why? Because you need woman . . .

HENRY: Oh God!

ADELA: Strong woman . . . like Soldadera . . .

HENRY *(Groaning)*: Oh God!

ADELA: She must kick your arse . . .

HENRY *(Deeper groan)*: Oh no.

(They are interrupted by the entrance of Solly and Rachel. Adela hurriedly goes back behind the counter.

Henry returns to his book, sandwich and coffee.

Solly, who is holding Rachel by the hand, stops just inside the doorway and looks around uncertainly. There is a brief whispered conversation between the two of them, after which Solly approaches the counter.

The moment Solly speaks, Henry looks up and stares at the couple. He continues to do so until their departure.)

SOLLY: Good evening, lady. Please . . . maybe you have got . . . tziken zup? You know it?

ADELA: What?

SOLLY: Tziken zup! . . .

ADELA: Henry! What's he want?

SOLLY *(To Henry)*: Tziken zup. Jewish tziken zup.

HENRY: With dumplings? Matzoh ball dumplings?

SOLLY: Yes. That is it . . . Jewish tziken zup! Thank you, mister.

(He turns back to Adela.)

ADELA: Tuesday today. Tuesday is vegetable soup day.

SOLLY: No tziken zup?

ADELA: Thursday is chicken soup. With noodles.

SOLLY: That is also good. Two tziken zups with noodles is also good . . . please.

ADELA: Not today. There is no chicken soup today. Only vegetable soup.

SOLLY: No tziken zup today?

ADELA: No.

(Solly murmurs conversation with Rachel, then turns back to Adela.)

SOLLY: What else you got, lady?

ADELA: I got chili. Beef and beans, tomatoes. You will like it.

SOLLY: You want we must eat chili? *(To Henry)* She wants we must eat chili!

ADELA: I make myself. Is very good. No?

SOLLY: No.

ADELA: Or something else. Plenty of sandwiches. Look . . . there's menu.

(She points to the menu on the wall. Solly has to put on spectacles to read it. He has a murmured conversation with Rachel.)

SOLLY *(To Adela)*: Thank you, lady, but no. *(To Henry)* Thank you, mister.

(Another whispered conversation between Solly and Rachel and then, with a last apologetic gesture and a nod to Henry and Adela, they leave.

Their departure has left a strange silence in the shop, with both Henry and Adela staring at the empty doorway.

Henry breaks the mood by taking his coffee cup to the counter for a refill.

He has a little mirthless smile and is shaking his head in disbelief. The interlude with Solly and Rachel has left him tense with suppressed excitement.)

HENRY: Amazing! Amazing!

ADELA: What is amazing?

HENRY: Those two . . . Yep! Quite simply amazing!

ADELA *(Puzzled)*: Why is amazing? Two old people.

HENRY: Two very lost old people from the look of things, don't you think? I wouldn't be surprised if I didn't get a "missing persons" card in my mail next week with their pictures on it. "Have You Seen Us?" Oh yes! I have not only seen them, my dear Adela, what is amazing is that I also happen to know them.

ADELA: You know them and you no say hello nicely?

HENRY: It's the voice I know. The man's voice. I know that voice. Oh yes! It has actually spoken to me before tonight.

ADELA *(Inviting him to say more)*: So, okay . . . Christmas. Just a month ago. Christmas Eve.

(He is still too self-absorbed to be clear about what he is saying.)

So what about it?

HENRY: We had a brief encounter. Those two old people and myself.

ADELA: Okay . . .

HENRY: And then just yesterday . . .

ADELA: You see them again?

HENRY: No . . . but then again . . . *(Another mirthless chuckle and head shaking)* . . . maybe I did!

ADELA *(Giving up)*: You talking nonsense, Henry.

HENRY *(Finally calming down, though still obviously inwardly very adrenalized)*: Please . . . let me start again. Last Christmas . . . Christmas Eve . . . you remember? . . . I came in here for my usual sandwich . . . in the course of which we played our wonderful little game once more.

ADELA: What game?

HENRY: Don't pretend you don't know. The little game you enjoy so much! You hate me and I hate you. That game. You played it so well that night I ended up leaving having taken only one bite out of my sandwich. Do you remember now?

ADELA *(Reluctantly)*: Maybe I remember.

HENRY: I ended up outside . . . standing under a lamppost a little further down . . . when those two . . . *(A gesture to the doorway, meaning Solly and Rachel)* . . . came walking past. They greeted me first, and because you made me feel so miserable, so fucking useless . . . I almost didn't hear them. But when it finally registered, I hurriedly greeted them back . . . and then . . . out of politeness . . . civilized decency, you know . . . I added to my greeting: ". . . and a happy Christmas to you!" They stopped . . . and do you know what he said?

ADELA: No.

HENRY: "Thank you . . . but we are Jews."

ADELA: So?

HENRY: What do you mean . . . "So?" So they were rebuking me for Christ's sake! All I had done was wish them a happy Christmas. How the hell was I supposed to know they were Jewish? I know I should have been "politically correct" and said "happy holidays," but for crying out aloud it was a knee-jerk reaction. I don't give a damn about Christmas anymore, but I grew up with it. There were no "happy holidays" in South Africa, just plain old "happy Christmas" and "Hark the Herald Angels" and all the rest of that charade of "Good Tidings to All Men." I want to vomit now whenever I hear a Christmas carol. When I called out to them last Christmas Eve I wasn't a crusading Christian. I was only trying to be friendly . . . extending a hand of goodwill. Maybe if you had not been such a bitch to me it wouldn't have upset me so much. But you had really made me feel utterly worthless that night, so when he responded to my simple good wishes . . . I don't know . . . it just added to what you had already done to me. It was one fucking rejection too many.

(Henry's obvious inner agitation is making Adela very nervous.
    Adela wants to say something but he silences her with an imperious gesture.)

But that is not the end of the story. Let me tell you about this morning.

(Pause . . . a change in tone.)

I had a wonderful, wonderful walk this morning, Adela. There's a little path next to the train tracks that take the Amtrak Surfliner all the way up to L.A. It's one of my favorite walks—because it goes right along the edge of the cliff . . . wonderful view of the sea and the beach below. God, it was beautiful this morning . . . blue sky, purple statice on the side of the path, white beach down below and then the sea stretching away endlessly to the horizon . . . Pacific . . . calm . . . as beautiful as a woman's smile. Drowning in it would have been a pleasure. But I didn't want to drown . . . I wanted to live! Yes, live!

(Change in mood) Today marked three months without a drink. Not bad, hey? There was actually something like hope in my heart . . . that maybe I would really be able to hang on this time . . . a feeling that maybe it was time to call this place where I have been living so grudgingly, so resentfully, that grubby, untidy little apartment of mine . . . maybe it was time to call it home. Sounds good, doesn't it?

ADELA: Sí.

HENRY: Now . . . to get back to my apartment I have to cross a large parking lot which is usually jam-packed with cars during the summer season. This morning it was empty. I was walking across it when, just by accident, I happened to look down at a certain moment and . . . there . . .

(He pauses. He needs to be calm; he is getting too excited again, and he wants to get it exactly right, exactly as it was, without any embellishment or emotional coloring.)

. . . There . . . gouged out in the tarmac surface in front of one of the parking bays, and obviously intended for the car and its occupants that had been parked there, was the Star of David . . . Do you know what that is, Adela?

(He goes to the chalkboard menu, wipes away what was written, then takes a piece of chalk and draws the Star of David.)

The Jewish Star of David . . . the one Hitler pinned on the clothes of little boys and girls, marking them down for the grand "Final Solution."

ADELA *(Reluctant nodding)*: Sí.

HENRY: And next to it, gouged out with the same precise and vicious determination, were three words.

(He writes on the menu chalkboard: "Fuck You Jew." [He does not speak them. Nobody in this play speaks them.]
Adela is now deeply disturbed by the way Henry is behaving. She raises her hands and waves them in front of her in rejection of the words he's written, then she turns around and starts to wipe the words away.)

ADELA: No, Henry. Is not good. No more. Please. No more.

HENRY *(Speaking with a violent authority that stops a suddenly frightened Adela)*: Yes more! Much more! Because I'm not finished.

(Pause.)

I dare not speak those words.

ADELA: No! You mustn't.

HENRY: Of course, I mustn't, but do you know why?

ADELA: Because it's ugly.

HENRY: Of course they're fucking ugly. We all know that. They're vile and poisonous. They were hammered out on the devil's anvil. But that is not why I mustn't say them. So fuck it and try again. Why—mustn't—I—say—them?

ADELA *(Now trying desperately to stop him)*: No! Is enough now, Henry! Borracho perdido is one thing but now you are becoming loco. You understand? ¡Locura! Mad! You must go, Henry. Go. Please . . . eat your sandwich and go.

HENRY *(No intention of leaving)*: Mad? Oh God, I wish I was. The truth, Adela, is I have never in my life been more sane and sober, seen myself more clearly than at this moment.

(Adela tries to launch into another outburst but Henry silences her with a "don't speak" gesture. He is suddenly very calm. He holds out a hand to her.)

Come . . . Please, Adela . . . Come sit with me at this table. Just for a few minutes . . . Let me explain . . . I am not mad, Adela . . . Just let me explain . . . Please . . .

(After a long pause, Adela sits very hesitantly. They sit facing each other at opposite ends of the table.)

Do you go to the movies?

ADELA: ¿El cine? Sí. The movies . . . yes.

HENRY: Sigourney Weaver? In a spaceship. *(She shakes her head uncertainly)* Macho lady with big gun and horrible alien. Big ugly monster inside her chest . . . horrible!!! Monster from another planet!

(Henry slowly stretches out his arm, his fingers curled to suggest the slime-dripping fangs of the beast in question—there is an expression on his face to match it.)

ADELA *(Beginning to understand)*: ¡Sí sí! Monstruo de otro planeta. *(She puts her hands over her eyes)* Monstruo is horrible. I no look at picture.

HENRY: Good, you've got it!

(Explaining very carefully. He points at his arm, which is still held out like the Alien *monster . . .)*

Now listen, this monster . . . what do you call it . . . monstruo? . . .

(He now points at the menu.)

Is those three words . . . and those three words . . .

(He now points at his own chest.)

. . . are inside me. Have always been inside me. Yes. They
are a part of my heritage as a South African. I don't know
how it was passed on to me, Adela—maybe they came in
with my mother's milk when she sang and suckled me at
her breast, or maybe there was some sort of evil spiritual
virus in the air I breathed when I was playing cowboys and
crooks as a little boy . . . and like a good South African
I caught it. But don't think I wasn't eventually aware of
what that benighted country could do to a human being
. . . how easily it could mutilate the innocence we are all
born with. So I fought it. That was one of the reasons
I ended up here in America with my family. I ended up
believing I had finally escaped it. I was wrong.

*(It is taking Adela a few seconds to understand what Henry
is saying. Henry goes through the cycle again—the monster,
the menu, himself—wordlessly. She eventually begins to understand.)*

ADELA: No, Henry.

HENRY: Yes, Henry! As I stood there looking down at that Star
and those three words . . . *(Speaks with a sense of profound
horror)* I heard them! I heard them inside me. And what
did I do? Put my foot on them as any decent human being
would have done and try to silence them? Obliterate
them? Or at least spit on them in denial? Or shed tears
on them for the centuries' load of suffering they carried?
No. I stared at them and the Star for what now feels like
an eternity . . . and then I simply walked away. I left it all
intact . . . for someone else to read!

(Pause.)

You understand now, Adela . . . it wasn't shock or disgust I felt when I stared at them, it was recognition. But what *was* erased on that walk back to my apartment was all the innocent beauty of the world that had so thrilled me a little earlier. All I could see on the walk back to my apartment was . . . *(Pointing at the menu board)* When our two friends . . . *(Pointing to the door)* . . . declined my innocent Christmas greeting a few months ago something stirred into life inside me . . . and when they walked in here tonight, there it was again . . . stirring inside me, trying to come out.

(Pause.)

What did you see when they walked in? Those two people. What did you see?

ADELA *(Puzzled by his question)*: Two old people . . . not American, I think . . . somewhere else.

HENRY: I saw Jews.

ADELA: Maybe.

HENRY: No maybe! I saw Jews! That's how it works, you see. I saw a walking illustration of anti-Semitic propaganda—the nose, the hunched back from bending over money bags . . . and, of course, matzoh ball soup . . .

(Neither of them see Solly and Rachel arrive in the doorway.)

The monster had got a name, you know. Prejudice! That's the name of the disease, my darling. And the symptoms are the same, whether it's Jew or black or coolie, that you happen to be looking at . . . hatred and fear of anything that is different. It's endemic to that beautiful country of mine. Like all decent liberal-minded men and women back there, I, of course, thought I had cured myself of it. Maybe others did. I hadn't. I'm rotten with it.

(Adela now sees Solly and Rachel.)

ADELA: Be quiet, Henry!

(She goes hurriedly to the menu board and makes sure that every last trace of what Henry wrote on it is erased.

Henry now registers the presence of Solly and Rachel. Solly looks back at him and smiles. Henry can't respond. He lowers his head and stares down at his half-eaten sandwich.)

SOLLY *(With a smile and a helpless gesture to Adela and Henry)*: No tziken zup anywhere!

(Once again, leaving an obviously nervous Rachel standing alone, he approaches the counter, making an apologetic gesture as he speaks to Adela.)

We find nothing . . .

(Pointing to the blank menu board.)

. . . and now you got nothing.

ADELA *(The voice of one eager to help)*: No . . . no . . . we got plenty of other things . . . just no . . . the soup you ask . . . but we got chili . . .

SOLLY: No . . . no chili . . .

ADELA: Okay . . . no chili . . . you right . . . I forget . . . no chili . . . but sandwiches . . . ham, beef, turkey . . . with onions, tomato . . . sprouts and lettuce . . . also jalapeño peppers . . . cheese . . .

SOLLY: No . . . no peppers . . . no cheese.

ADELA: Sí . . . Okay, no peppers . . . but ham, beef and turkey . . .

SOLLY: Vegetable soup.

ADELA: No vegetable soup. Vegetable soup is finished.

(Solly and Rachel stare at each other in silence for a few seconds.)

Ham, beef, turkey . . .

SOLLY: No . . . also no ham . . . thank you.

(He looks back anxiously at Rachel. She is showing signs of desperation. He turns back to Adela.)

Turkey is good.

ADELA *(Taking it as a question)*: Turkey is okay . . . is very good . . . fresh . . . today . . .

SOLLY: Two.

ADELA: No peppers . . . okay?

SOLLY: No peppers is okay. And no cheese.

ADELA: Pickle?

SOLLY: Yes. We like pickle.

ADELA: Go sit. I bring it to you.

(Solly goes back to Rachel. A nod and a smile at the still-lowered head of Henry as Solly passes him. A few whispered exchanges with Rachel, after which he takes her arm and, whispering softly, leads her to a table. The image is one of deep and protective love.

A strained silence in the shop as Adela starts to make the sandwiches. She tries to ease the tension by switching on the radio. Mariachi music comes over the airwaves. Watching the other three anxiously, Adela hums along with the music. Solly joins her by softly clapping out the rhythm of the music.

Henry creates the pretense of reading. Solly watches him and nods approvingly. He whispers something to Rachel and points at Henry. Rachel looks at him nervously.)

SOLLY *(To Henry)*: That is a good book I think.

HENRY *(Without looking up)*: It's okay.

SOLLY: I also think you have got many books.

(Pause.)

Is it so?

HENRY: Quite a few.

SOLLY: And you read them all?

HENRY: Yes.

(Adela brings the sandwiches to their table.)

SOLLY *(Smiling at Adela)*: A sheynem dank!

ADELA *(Turning to Henry for help)*: Henry, what's he saying?

HENRY: I think the gentleman is saying, "Thank you."

SOLLY: Yes . . . yes . . . "Thank you."

ADELA *(To Solly)*: Anything else? You want anything else?

SOLLY: No, thank you.

(Adela returns to the counter. Solly turns again to Henry.)

You speak Yiddish, mister?

HENRY: No.

(Henry goes back to his book.)

SOLLY *(Wagging a loving finger at Henry)*: Just like Aaron! *(Nudging Rachel and pointing at Henry)* You see him. In the book again. Just like Aaron.

(Solly goes to work on the two sandwiches, carefully rearranging them. That done, he places one of them in front of Rachel. In a whispered voice he urges her to eat. Rachel shakes her head. Solly tries again and, this time, after looking around to make sure that no one is paying any attention to them, he sings very softly the Hebrew song: "Mejerke Mein Suhn":)

Mejerke mein suhn
Mejerke mein suhn
Oi Mejerke mein suhn
Zi weiss tu, var wemen du steihst?
Lifnei Melech Malchei hamlochim, Tatunju.

(Mejerke my son
Mejerke my son
Oy Mejerke my son
Do you know before whom you stand?
Before Him, King of kings, the only King, my Father.)

(All his attention is focused on Rachel, whose agitation gradu-
ally subsides. Even with the radio going Henry can hear Solly's
singing. After a few seconds he gestures to Adela to turn off the
radio. She does. At the end of the singing Rachel wipes away a
tear and starts to eat.)

(Now conscious of Henry, who is staring at them) Rabbi says
it is good for her. "Solomon," he says to me, "let her cry
if she wants. If it helps her to eat then it is good for her."
HENRY: What were you singing?
SOLLY: Just an old Jewish song.
HENRY: What do the words mean?
SOLLY: The words? Yiddish words.
HENRY: Yes. But what do they mean? What is the song about?

(Solly, satisfying himself that Rachel is trying to deal with her
sandwich, turns to Henry.)

SOLLY: It's Aaron, you see. Our son. I use to sing it with him.
Before we eat. While Mama is getting the food, me and
Aaron use to sing. But now I sing it for her because . . .
our Aaron is gone.
HENRY: Gone?

SOLLY *(Shaking his head with a finger to his lips to indicate Henry mustn't ask that question)*: Please, mister . . . Rachel . . .

HENRY: But the words. Please tell me what the words mean?

SOLLY: In the song I ask my son what he wants and he tells me. He wants children, a long life and his bread. "But why the children?" I ask him. And he says so that he can teach them the Torah. "And the long life?" I ask him. And he tells me so that he can sing praises to the Lord. "But what about the bread?" I ask him. And he says to me: "Bless the bread, Papa."

HENRY: Sing it again.

SOLLY *(Embarrassed)*: No . . . no . . . it is not good.

HENRY: Please . . . it's just us in here . . . it was very beautiful.

(Adela, having used the excuse of bringing more coffee to the table, is listening to the conversation between the two men, prepared to intervene if necessary.)

ADELA: Yes. Please sing. Henry is right. We want to hear.

(After some hesitation, Solly talks to Rachel again in an undertone. A frightened Rachel looks at Henry and Adela. She shakes her head, Solly persists quietly, and eventually Rachel calms down.

Tapping out a rhythm on the table, Solly and Rachel sing. This time we clearly hear the words and Solly's cracked and tired old voice. Henry and Adela listen quietly. When Solly and Rachel are finished singing, there are a few seconds of complete silence in the shop. Solly and Rachel quietly eat their sandwiches.

Adela goes back behind the counter and starts clearing up.

Henry pushes his sandwich aside, places his bookmark back in the book, and then stands up. He is trying to leave but something is restraining him. Solly, sensing Henry's dilemma, looks up at him. Henry sits down again and stares at Solly, who stares back.)

HENRY: Forgive me.

(*A questioning gesture from Solly.*)

Please forgive *me*.

(*Pause.*)

SOLLY (*Nodding his head slowly*): Of course I forgive you. What
    did you do?
HENRY: I hated you.
SOLLY: I know.

(*Pause. They look unflinchingly into each other's eyes.*)

But why?
HENRY: You were ugly . . . you were a Jew . . .
SOLLY: I still am.

(*A pause. Henry is shaking his head in denial.*)

Speak. I will listen.
HENRY (*After a gesture of utter helplessness*): I don't know . . . now
    you are beautiful . . . I . . . love you.
SOLLY: Then God will also forgive you.

(*Solly nods and turns back to Rachel and they eat their sandwiches. After a few more seconds of silence, Henry gets up and
leaves the shop.*)

Epilogue

Henry returns to his position under the street light from the start of the play. The sandwich shop is dimly lit in the background. Adela is behind the counter and Solly and Rachel at their table.

He again speaks directly to the audience:

HENRY: I didn't know when I walked out of the sandwich shop
that I wasn't going to see any of them again. All I knew
in the silence that followed Solly's last statement was that
there was nothing more I wanted to say . . . nothing more
I could say . . . nothing more I should say. Even a simple "good night" or just a parting wave to Adela would
somehow have violated that moment and the mysterious
emptiness of it. I knew it for what it was and it was mine.
I wasn't going to touch it with words. All I can tell you for
sure is that the journey from hate to love was the shortest
one my heart has ever made. When I walked out . . . all my
dominoes were down. My one regret about that moment,
though, is that it also involved losing Adela. When I went

back to the shop two weeks later it was shut and there was a "to let" sign in the window. You see, my encounter with Solly and Rachel didn't need a sequel . . . it was complete unto itself. But there could have been some sort of follow-up with Adela, don't you think? I was prepared for it, wanted it, in fact, when I went back to the shop two weeks later. I had my favorite recording of Kathleen Ferrier in my pocket: "Blow the Wind Southerly." I wanted to give it to her. Would have been a good story, don't you think . . . two bitter adversaries ending up as good friends? I felt so cheated as I stood outside staring in at our old battleground—everything was gutted. After all, being the two misfits we were, we had earned each other, don't you think? All those insults we had traded had laid the foundations for a real friendship . . . I did make a few attempts to track her down . . . but without a photograph I couldn't even try to find her with one of these . . .

(He takes out the card in his book.)

It's my one and only souvenir of Adela, and what happened to me that night. Remember it? "Have You Seen Us?"

It's a good question. I like to believe I did.

Anyway . . . there it is. Good night and . . . happy holidays!

(He leaves.)

END OF PLAY

Glossary

By Marianne McDonald

ABAFAZI	Dead man
AG	"Ah"
AIKONA	Expression of dismay, "No, you're wrong," "I disagree"
AKKERS	Fields, plots
AMADODA	Dead woman
AMAGINTSA	Hoods, hoodlums that go in gangs
AMANGCWABA	Graves
BAAS	Boss
BAASIE	Little master
BAKKIE/ FLENTER BAKKIE	Wreck of a truck
BANTU	Black people, covering six hundred ethnic groups in Central to Southern Africa
BILTONG	Jerky
BLOEKOMBOOM	Blue gum tree

BOEREWORS	Farmer's sausage
BOER PAMPOENS	Pumpkins
BOKKIE	Nickname: "Little Springbok"
BOONTJIES	Beans
COLOREDS	One of four official racial categories (along with whites, blacks and Asians) of the "old" South Africa; "Colored" is defined as anyone of mixed racial descent
DEURMEKAAR	Confused, out of one's head
DOEK	Headscarf
DOM	Stupid
DONNER	Curse word: "Bastard"
ERTJIES	Peas
EWE	"Yes"
EWE, JA, DIS TWEE . . .	"Yes, that's it, two times . . ." (referring to a grave that's been dug up)
EWE . . . ZIMBINI . . . IS TWEE	"Look . . . that's it . . . two bodies"
FINISH AND KLAAR/KLAAR	All over, that's it, to sum it up
GAT	Fishing hole, pond
GATSRIVIER	Intermittent stream
GRAAFF-REINET	Village near Nieu Bethesda
HAAI	"Yes"
HANEPOOT KORRELS	Muscat grape, often used in jams
HOKKIE	Tiny place
IKHAYA	Home
INDUDUMO	Thunder

INGCWABA	Grave, mispronounced as "ingiwaba" by Visagie
INKWENKWANA	Kid, boy
iWANDLE	Whitecap of a wave
JA	"Yes"
KAALGAT	Naked
KAK	Shit
KAROO	A vast semi-desert region in the heart of South Africa; "karoo" is a Khoi word meaning "place of little water"; few plants grow on the dry mountains, but farms thrive in the valleys and lowlands
KLOOF	Chasm, gap
KOM, MAN	"Come on, man"
KOPPIE	Hill in South Africa
LEKKER	Delicious
LIEFLING	Darling, sweetheart
MARIE biscuits	Vanilla tea biscuits
MOEG	Tired
MOS	"You know," "Indeed"
OUMA	Grandma
OUPA	Grampa
OUTJIE	Little fellow
PASOP, WITMAN	"Be careful, whiteman"
POLISIE	Police
PONDOK	Shack, made with whatever is available
POPPIE	Doll, little darling girl; disparaging way to refer to a woman

RUMATIEK	Rheumatism
SHEBEEN	Bar where illegal alcohol is sold
SKELM	Crook
SKINNER	Gossip
SKINNERING	Gossiping
SNOT EN TRANE	Tears and snot
SPOKE	Ghosts ("spook" is "ghost")
STEENBRAS	Delicious lagoon fish
STOMPIE	Stump, such as a short candle
S'TRUES GOD	"I swear by God"
SUGA WENA	"Fuck off"
TORTELDUIFIE	Turtledove
TRALIES	Latticework, railings
TSOTSI	Hoodlums, often young gang boys
UMFAZI	Married woman
THE VALLEY	A fertile valley deep in the Sneeuberg; fruits, vegetables and alfalfa are produced there
VELD	Open rural spaces: grassy, or with low scrub and bushes, grazing areas
THE VILLAGE	The small town of Nieu Bethesda
VOETSEK, WITMAN	"Fuck off, white man"
WAAR	True
WAT IS	What is
WENA	Go
WRAGTY	Really
ZIMBINI, ZIMBINI, ZIMBINI	Bodies, bodies, bodies

Afterword

By Marianne McDonald

The three plays in this volume: *Coming Home* (2009), *Have You Seen Us?* (2009) and *The Train Driver* (2010) are the final three in what Athol Fugard regards as defining the arc of his fifty-year-long writing career, which began in 1961 with *Blood Knot.* He continues to write, but these plays determine his approach to documenting the experiences of the undocumented, and giving a voice to the voiceless. He tells the stories of his country and himself. These plays also trace the history of South Africa from the beginning of apartheid (1948) to Nelson Mandela becoming president in the first free election in 1994. Beginning in 1995, the Truth and Reconciliation Commission tried to provide some catharsis to the people for the brutalities of apartheid.

Veronica in *Coming Home* is as much a victim as Pumla Lolwana in *The Train Driver*, both forgotten dropouts from the new and "better" South Africa, which does not treat its AIDS victims properly, nor provide adequate care for the impoverished homeless. *Coming Home* is a continuation of *Valley Song* (1995). *Valley Song* was filled with hope, but *Com-*

ing Home expresses some of the despair that comes from little or no change of the abuses, only who commits them.

Coming Home takes place in the new South Africa, in which many of the dreams have turned into nightmares. Good education is rarely available, and classes are often taught by inadequate, drunken teachers. There is not enough employment; there are still segregated areas; terrible hospital care; AIDS is rampant with little medication available; drugs and alcoholism are a way of life, along with the crime needed to sustain these habits, so robberies, murders and rapes plague the new South Africa. The poverty is now worse than it was even in the apartheid years, mainly from corruption in both the central and local governments. There are riots against the "foreigners," particularly skilled laborers from Nigeria, Zimbabwe and Mozambique. Many are "necklaced" in the way traitors were under apartheid (an automobile tire circles the neck of the victim, gasoline poured over, then set alight). Young people face a bleak future. Whites are often treated as second-class citizens and not given jobs, so discrimination has not been eradicated, it has only changed targets.

There are many gains, including much foreign business and investments. Nevertheless, not enough economic equity has been put into practice. There is now a wealthy black and Colored middle and upper class. The rights that appear in the constitution should be the envy of the free world, but the reality is very different.

At present Nieu Bethesda has many empty houses, but the prices have gone up. Many people have died of AIDS and there is much crime in Pienaarsig (the Colored area which is de facto segregated). In the rest of the village the houses are regularly burgled, and the police simply don't answer alarms or calls. Yet, life goes on, and it can be hopeful as it is in *Coming Home* or dire as it is in *Victory* (2007).

Coming Home is bittersweet. The dreams one had for Veronica have been exchanged for the grim reality of this new

South Africa. But she comes home to begin dreaming again, accompanied by a miracle to match Oupa's: but where his white seeds had produced big fat white pumpkins, her seed has produced a little boy. Locating a future for her son, Mannetjie, through Alfred, her former friend, is her expiation of the guilt of abandoning her child, because she is dying from AIDS.

Grandpa's loving hand is seen not only for the legacy of appreciating life that he leaves behind, but also in the inheritance that will pay for his great-grandson's education. It seems he will be a storyteller, a writer who will tell the tales of his people: local stories that speak also to human universals.

Mistakes are made: Alfred stole from Veronica, but he repents and is very sorry for what he did. He makes up for it by giving nothing less than his future life, returning what he stole, and rectifying his mistake by caring for dying Veronica and looking after her child. This shows the capacity of human beings to do good in the world. It is an affirmation of hope in the new South Africa, in its main resource, its people. We see Veronica never giving up, singing in her heart, as we remember from *Valley Song*. The two songs she sings in the course of the play delight Alfred (and the audience), as they used to delight her oupa.

The creative artist is a frequent theme in Fugard's plays. Here, the artist, Oupa, uses the earth as his palette. He remains a guardian angel for all of them, and gives Alfred invaluable lessons about appreciating the miracle of life as told by the seeds. He appears at the end of the play, giving his lessons of life and death and miracles directly to his grandchild, through the image of the turtledove singing the return of spring. What made him happy just before he died was Alfred showing him a little green pumpkin plant that survived the destructive frost of an overlong winter. Likewise, Mannetijie is the lone survivor in his family, a fragile young life, and also a miracle. Oupa is both a ghost (the first ghost seen in a Fugard play) and a muse. That leads to Mannetjie's line at the end of the play: "Oupa's . . . Fan . . . tas . . . tic . . . Mir . . . acle." There is a continuity of generations: as Oupa planted his crops, Mannetjie will plant his seeds, namely words on the blank page.

Lessons are taught by death, and its part in the cycle of life and rebirth. This is all part of God's plan, which is unintelligible, as Oupa points out. Trust. One has to take the good with the bad, and learn to survive, and have hope. One can still count on new life that follows the old, and the occasional generosity of human beings. This play has some of the same sobering messages of the pitfalls that could entrap young women in Nieu Bethesda, and the new South Africa; brutal realities are succeeded by hope and redemption for them all through human compassion.

Fugard's plays not only indict South Africa, but any countries in which prejudice and abuse operate. *Have You Seen Us?* shows us Henry Parsons, an Afrikaner and academic, who lives in self-exile in California. Fugard dealt with academics in other plays, as he did in *Sorrows and Rejoicings*, also about an exiled South African (Dawid Olivier), who taught literature, and suffered from alcoholism.

Parsons tries to escape his mutilating South African heritage of prejudice, but finds he shares it with some Americans who see Hispanics and Jews through the distorting lens of racial stereotype. (In his plays, Fugard removes the masks of superiority, which often cover an intense feeling of inferiority.)

Have You Seen Us? is Fugard's first play set in California. Fugard is dealing with another experience he had himself: having read a hate message against Jews in a parking lot. The characters are fictional, but based on Fugard's past: he also is from South Africa, also was an alcoholic and nearly lost his family as a result, until he gained sobriety in 1983. He, like our hero, has one daughter. He also grew up with hate and prejudice, as outlined in *"Master Harold" . . . and the boys* (1982). How that hate turned to love, he says, is a most mysterious process. That is what he tries to describe in this play: the indescribable.

There are classical Greek Tragedy influences (as usual in a Fugard play), from the number of actors (three), to the same themes. Music is also ever-present, as in Fugard's own life, as a source of strength and sanity (besides a mine of memories). Fugard has said that music has always shaped his writing.

He traces the past of his characters: for instance, the waitress, Adela Venegas, whose grandmother was a heroine (Soldadera) in Mexico, has her grandmother's same feistiness. She is based on the many Mexicans in Southern California whom Fugard saw discriminated against by the law, and exploited in low-paying jobs, which help sustain the California economy for the benefit of others.

Fugard took some names from people he knew and befriended in California, such as Ignacio Venegas, who helped him with his Spanish, shared some of the details of being an immigrant from Mexico, and provided words for some of the songs. Genoveva Bobadilla told him about her village life in Mexico.

Have You Seen Us? investigates the loneliness and occasional despair of immigrants. It shows their vulnerability when they must live with foreigners (the native of their new country) who do not understand them and are prejudiced against them because they are believed to deprive them of jobs, or because they think differently. This is another theme that is as old as antiquity, when, for instance, the fifth-century B.C. Greeks exercised their prejudice against the "barbarians," whom they enslaved whenever they defeated them in wars. In Euripides' *Phoenician Women* (ca. 409 B.C.), Eteocles, one of Oedipus' sons (of the ruling family of Thebes), is forced into exile. He tells his mother, Jocasta that one of his worst losses is not having free speech. In Fugard's play, the rude Henry bullies Adela into serving him what he wants, by threatening to call the immigration authorities about her. He rightly suspects that she might be illegal, which is verified by the speed of her capitulation. Adela, too, is deprived of free speech or, at least free action, in this context, and is forced to obey an abusive customer.

Sometimes the worst comes about when the prejudices of the original country and the host country match, as they do here between the South African immigrant and his American hosts. The title *Have You Seen Us?* refers to missing people, but is more ominous. Many people are kidnapped, robbed, raped or murdered but, in the case of immigrants, they often vanish without a trace.

Fugard has often said he saves and tells stories of people who cannot tell their own. Here again he is telling stories about the disappeared, expressly immigrants, who can easily vanish, and who are often ignored by their host country, their rights severely compromised or unacknowledged. Yet his plays are never "message" plays—they are far too complicated and artful for that.

At the end of the play, Parsons asks, "Have you seen us?" By asking the audience this question he seems to be asking, "Have you seen yourself?" Fugard holds a mirror up to society, and not only the audience's prejudices, but also the things they are not used to seeing: namely who they are. This is the task of all good theatre.

Fugard has tracked a perilous voyage from hate to love, suggesting in his usual hopeful way, that when love turns to hate it can stay there or foster more. However, when hate turns to love, there is hope of salvation. Maybe there is a way we can all be forgiven for what we have blindly hated, as when the Jewish Solly tells Henry that God will forgive him for his prejudice. At the end, besides loving Adela and Solly (his "enemies") he may indeed regain the self-love that turned to self-hatred through his years as an alcoholic.

In *The Train Driver*, Roelf (Roofie) Visagie is a white Afrikaner,
a train driver, who ran over a despairing black woman, Pumla
Lomla. Fugard is once again dealing with the new South
Africa, as he does in *Victory* and *Coming Home*, both set in Nieu
Bethesda. Here the location has shifted to Port Elizabeth, his
earlier home before he acquired a house in Nieu Bethesda.

In discussing this play at a rehearsal, Fugard said it is a
culmination of the sense of white guilt he had, followed by a
symbolic catharsis of Roelf (his stand-in in the play). In a symbolic moment representing what Fugard tried to do with all
his writing, he claims the nameless as his own, and acknowl-
edges the guilt that comes from hurting others as his own personal train hurtled ahead.

Fugard has said that from the moment he saw it, he has
always admired and been influenced by Kon Ichikawa's 1956
film, *The Burmese Harp*, which showed a corporal Mizushima,
who alone survives the loss of his men when they refuse to surrender to the British. Dressed as a Buddhist monk, Mizushima
then decides to stay in Burma and bury bodies. He redeems
his life by his mission, the same way that Roelf does: both
were driven slightly mad by the senseless deaths they were
forced to face, and by burying the bodies of both friends and
enemies rotting on the battlefield.

Roelf goes to where the victim might have been buried.
He realizes that Simon's suggestion to bury the new body as if
it were the body of Red Doek (the name Roelf gives the nameless woman after the red scarf she was wearing) would be just
the catharsis he finally needs to forgive himself and reconcile
himself with God. Roelf realizes, at last, who he is and also
recognizes Simon for who he is, and who his people are. Roofie's rose-colored glasses of white privilege have fallen away.

As in so many of Fugard's plays, hope figures prominently:
Roelf realizes that this mother decided on suicide for herself

and her child because her hope had run out. At the end Simon is rewarded for his compassion toward Roelf (realizing full well his own life was at risk) by losing his job and his shovel at the same time. He denies to the police that he knew Roelf (like Peter in the Bible, both deny knowing their brother). The amagintsa might not be so easily deceived, and there is always the danger they might return for Simon. It is a bleak future looming for Simon.

In spite of the awful conditions for some, we see that the treasure of the country is still in the good human beings who live there. But they will have to overcome the ignorance that has led to racism on all sides of the color spectrum.

This is a play about white guilt, the suffering of the people of color, existential angst, the angst of South Africa itself trying to live down its past while it stumbles into its future. Fugard shows us that they are on a collision course. Truth will need reconciliation before it is too late.

Simon, holding out his hands at the end is a way to show he must learn to receive, but also create, his singular talent of giving in his own way. Here that gesture is altered to show a type of hopelessness. By this final gesture, Simon shows his greatest loss. As do all good plays, this informs and indicts the audience.

All three plays deal with the ends of lives, guilt and potential redemption through compassion. They engage the emotions and the minds of all those fortunate enough to see a performance, so that just as Mr. M said in *My Children! My Africa!*:

> If the struggle needs weapons, give it words, Thami. Stones and petrol bombs can't get inside those armored cars. Words can. They can do something even more devastating than that . . . they can get inside the heads of those inside the armored cars. I

speak to you like this because if I have faith in anything, it is faith in the power of the word. Like my
master, the great Confucius, I believe that, using only
words, a man can right a wrong and judge and execute
the wrongdoer. You are meant to use words like that.

MARIANNE MCDONALD, PhD, MRIA, Professor of Classics and Theatre, UCSD, is a writer and translator, whose work has been produced
internationally. Her latest play is called *Peace*, about a dysfunctional
Irish alcoholic family. She has lived in South Africa and worked with
Athol Fugard for many years. This has resulted in the most complete
book on Fugard's work: *Space, Time, and Silence: The Craft of Athol Fugard*.
http://mariannemcdonald.net/

Pages from a Notebook

(2000)

Athol Fugard

June 11

I woke up this morning on the coast of Southern California to an overcast gray day and my seventieth birthday. I feel good about it. It comes after a lunatic year in which I directed five productions of my play *Sorrows and Rejoicings* on three continents—an exercise that lived up to the title of the play in every sense of the word. It left me physically and emotionally drained and made it very easy for me at the end of it to decide that my days as a director were over in much the same way that I decided a few years ago that I would not do any more acting. I have no doubts about those decisions. I've never had much of an opinion of myself in either of those two roles. They had been forced on me in my early years of making theatre in South Africa when I discovered that no one wanted to touch the plays that I wanted to write. I had no choice really but to get up there and have a go at it myself. What surprises me is that I stayed up there for so long, because I don't think I have the right temperament for either acting or directing.

There are a few other resolutions as well and, taken together, they have given me a sense of adventure as I face up to whatever time is left to me, but now without any clutter to my essential identity as a writer. I've reinforced that sense of adventure by replacing the rickety old table I've been working on up to now with a beautiful, solid slab of mahogany on four legs—my new "home"—the safest place in my universe because when I sit here I know with something approaching conviction who and what I am.

That year of rehearsal rooms and nerve-wrecking and depressing openings (I never did learn how to cope with them!) gave me no chance to write. All I could do, in the succession of hotel rooms I lived in, was a few vacuous entries in this notebook and a lot of yearning for the time when I would be free once again to explore that ultimate terra incognita, that most outer of all outer spaces—the blank page.

So here it is, the moment I anticipated so longingly during that muscle-cramping year, and the question of course is: What now? It's not an intimidating question. I don't think there has ever been a time when I didn't have at least half a dozen stories that I knew I had to tell sooner or later. I could page back through this notebook and find many entries short-listing the "appointments I have to keep." The trouble is that, without exception, it has never been left to me to decide when that should be. Nothing would make me happier than to make this the moment when I settle down to telling the story of a hot summer's afternoon I spent with my dear (and now dead) friend Barney Simon in the garden of The Ashram—my Port Elizabeth home—watching birds and talking about our lives and work. It would be a celebration of one of the abiding passions of my life—bird-watching—and one of my most important friendships. But this is not its moment because it's the story of Pumla Lolwana that is commanding my attention this morning. It is just over a year and a half since I read about her and her three children for the first time. When I first read

about her, I immediately recognized hers as one of those stories
I would have an appointment with some day. This is what I read:

December 12, 2000

MOTHER AND THREE CHILDREN DIE IN TRACK SUICIDE
OWN CORRESPONDENT, CAPE TOWN, TUESDAY

A mother with a child on her back and two toddlers
in her arms stood on the tracks in front of an oncoming train—and when the five-year-old child tried to
scurry away, she pulled him back before the family
was pulverized under the train's wheels, *Die Burger*
newspaper reported.

The seriously traumatized train driver looked on
helplessly as Pumla Lolwana (thirty-five), from the
Samora Machel squatter camp, and her three children: Lindani (two), Andile (three) and Sesanda (five),
died on the railway line between Philippi and Nyanga
on the Cape Flats on Friday afternoon.

By Monday night nobody had claimed the bodies
of the mother and her three children from the Salt
River mortuary. The reason for her suicide, barely
two weeks before Christmas, still remains a mystery.

Metrorail confirmed to *Die Burger* that Lolwana
apparently committed suicide. "The train driver is
receiving counseling. He is extremely traumatized,
because he saw the drama play out in front of him
and wasn't able to stop the train in time," Metrorail
representative Daphne Kayster said.

An industrial social worker who works with train
drivers told *Die Burger* that many people use suicide
in front of oncoming suburban trains as their "way
out" when personal problems get too much.

Statistics published at the beginning of this month
indicate that approximately four hundred people die

on the train tracks between Cape Town and Khayelitsha every year.

According to an eyewitness, one of the children
managed to escape from his mother's arms. However,
she pulled him back and held tightly on to him while
the train sped closer. She made no attempt to get
away or save her children.

Jaqueline van Rensburg, industrial social worker,
who treats up to fifteen train drivers a month after
accidents, told *Die Burger* that the drivers work under
extremely difficult circumstances and feel guilty
whenever anybody dies under their train.

"The drivers feel very guilty because they have
absolutely no control over the train. A train needs
up to three hundred meters to come to a stop. They
can't swerve. They very much want to prevent the
accident, but they are powerless.

"Some of the train drivers whom I have spoken
to say they always wonder about the victim's families
and put themselves in that person's shoes. In the long
term these incidents have a negative impact on train
drivers."

The original is a file in my computer: I read the story in the
internet edition of the *Mail&Guardian*. I have now copied it
out, word for word by hand, into this notebook. I did that
because I feel the need to possess it at a very personal level,
to make it a part of my life. Having done that I ask myself,
yet again: This moment of "recognition" that has been such
a recurring experience in my writing life . . . What is it all
about? How does it work? Why is it that certain stories, faces
or incidents from the thousands that crowd my daily life will
separate themselves from the others and take on an imperative
quality that demands that I deal with them and, in my case,
that obviously means writing about them.

In 1988, at a time when reports of the latest horrors of apartheid were crowding out each other on the front pages of our local Port Elizabeth newspaper, it was a little three-inch item hidden away on the back pages that really stopped me and made me read it again and then again. The headline story on the front page was about the massacre of twenty people when the police opened fire on a funeral procession of a political activist. I, of course, read it and was horrified, but I moved on until I came to the story of Anela Myalatya, a school teacher in a small country town, who had been necklaced [a form of torture when a tire is hung around someone's neck, doused with gasoline and then lit on fire] by an angry mob because the word had gone around that he was an informer. After reading it several times, I fetched a pair of scissors, cut it out and pasted it into my notebook. Is it as simple as Stalin's cynical remark that a thousand deaths are a statistic and one death a tragedy? That, of course, is what a writer is always looking for—a strong story with an unhappy ending. In my case, however, I know that there is also something else at work, something less easy to define. It involves one of my more important instincts as a writer, because *it* has chosen the stories I decided to tell. What I recognized in that image, face, incident or three-inch newspaper story that stopped me, is that it held out the possibility of looking at something in myself even though in most cases I was not aware of this at the time. Only afterward did I realize that these stories, these images, were a shield I had held up so that I could slay a private Medusa.

That was certainly the case with Anela Myalatya. *My Children! My Africa!*, the play I went on to write based on that three-inch item in the newspaper, is a very political statement about a moment in my country's history, but also an intensely personal one. I have correctly described Mr. M (the school teacher in my play) as an attempt at self-portraiture. His passions for learning and language, his belief in evolution rather than violent revolution . . . all of those faiths and qualities,

as well as his serious flaws, are mine. I was not consciously
aware of any of this when I started writing the play. In fact, if
I had had the deliberate intention of doing that, I doubt very
much if that play or any of the others would have been written. Those "intentions" are secrets that must be kept from
even the writer himself.

So this morning it is Pumla Lolwana's story that I will try
to live with. Somewhere in his writing, Rilke advises a young
poet to strive for a degree of innocence when he confronts
blank paper and the start of a new adventure. I am not young,
and innocence is hard to come (by now)—so many words on
paper lie behind this moment!—but I know it is good advice
and I will try as hard as I can to follow it. In this instance I am
certainly innocent of intentions or expectations. I don't know
what will come, if anything, out of that newspaper story.

JUNE 13

My usual sunset walk along the beach in the late afternoon
and, for a change, the sky was clear; at this time of the year the
sun usually sets behind a bank of fog, which waits far out on
the horizon to come drifting in during the night. After a few
days of strong spring tides and heavy surf, the sea was again
very calm with hardly enough energy in it to uncurl a few
small waves close inshore. In the two years that I've been here
I've never seen a really wild sea like the ones I grew up with
on the Eastern Cape of South Africa, when South Atlantic
gales lashed the coast. Halfway along my walk I did something
that doesn't come easily to me in America: I switched off my
neurotic obsession with time, which in this instance meant
regulating my walk so that I would be back in time for one of
the major items in my daily schedule—the BBC World News
broadcast at six P.M. Instead I sat down on the sand with no
other intention than to watch the setting sun. The last time

I did that was in the Karoo, in Nieu Bethesda, on my walks in the koppies around the village when I would choose a convenient sun-warmed rock and sit down and let time pass, just "be" (to the extent that my restless nature is capable of that meditative state).

Here on the beach, as so many times in the Karoo, it was a gentle breeze, this one off the sea, playing on my skin, which turned the mystery of time and its passing into a physical experience. The sunset was simple and serene—a huge smoky orange globe trailing a wake of golden light on the sea as it dropped slowly to the horizon. I started thinking about Pumla Lolwana again.

The morning session at my table had started off with another close reading of the newspaper story. I took up each sentence and looked at it as carefully as I do the beautiful wave-polished pebbles I pick up on my beach walks. And, just as I do them, I held on to each sentence for a few seconds, turning it over and over, so as to examine it still more carefully before putting it back in its place on the page and moving on. The one sentence I couldn't let go of easily, that I kept going back to and looking at again and again was the opening one:

> A mother with a child on her back and two toddlers in her arms stood on the tracks in front of an oncoming train—and when the five-year-old child tried to scurry away, she pulled him back before the family was pulverized under the train's wheels.

My mind stumbled and fell over itself in trying to deal with that sentence. No matter how hard I tried I couldn't take it in, truly understand it in a way that made it possible for me to move on. Was it because I couldn't "see" it? The sentence is profoundly disturbing, it has a fierce energy in it, but when I tried to turn it into a picture, my mind refused to move, all it could do was stare at the horror of it. Because the idea alone—a mother commits suicide and kills her three children with herself—is not enough for me as a writer. Ideas never have been. Some sort of picture or image has been the starting point to everything I have written and I need one now if I am going to do something with that newspaper report, but try as I may I can't break the paralyzing effect of that sentence. Pumla Lolwana is shrouded in a darkness my imagination can't penetrate. I've tried to unblock it by imagining the sound of those few dreadful seconds: the children's cries, especially the little boy struggling to get away, because he knew what his mother was trying to do, and their names, their beautiful names! Surely she called them out when she tried to comfort and calm them as the train got closer, and then the noise of the train itself, the hooter, the screech of brakes . . . but even that ploy didn't work.

I went through the story again hoping I might have overlooked something that would set me off, but it was a pointless exercise; I already knew the story by heart and I knew there wasn't anything that would help me start to build a picture of her. With a growing sense of frustration I put her aside and turned to other work.

Sitting there on the beach at the end of the day, watching the sky fade through a spectrum of soft pastel colors, I had to ask myself why my imagination wasn't working for me this time. Why wasn't it taking control of the facts as laid out in the newspaper story, and creating a plausible fiction as it had done so many times in my past fifty years of writing. I'd never known it to hesitate in that way before. Why now? Was it that it felt it didn't have the right—that much vaunted writer's liberty and license—to do that this time? Why not just go back to my table tonight and, in exactly the same way as I put the school teacher of that three-inch newspaper story into a tired old double-breasted suit in my imagination, see that young mother standing there on the tracks waiting for the train *barefoot*? That one little detail might be the trigger I was looking for.

That little surge of hope didn't last long. I had a growing sense that in fact this time I was without any rights to liberty or license. Apart from the fact that suicide is something I know I will never understand, will always be a mystery to me, there is something about the story of Pumla Lolwana and her three children that would make feeding it to my writer's ego very obscene.

As for just witnessing it . . . I can't even do that, because I don't in fact know if she was wearing shoes or if she and the children were barefoot.

JUNE 14

As an alternative to the beach, I sometimes walk next to the railway line that connects San Diego to Los Angeles. The regular traffic on this line is the blue-and-white Coaster, a local suburban commuter train with a blaring organlike note for a hooter, and, less frequently, the blue-and-silver Surfliner, which goes with only a few stops all the way to Los Angeles. A few times during the day and night, long freight trains also travel along this line. I saw a real beauty yesterday: forty-five-coaches-and-wagons-long, and all with the name Barnum & Bailey Circus proudly emblazoned on their sides.

The walk is a lovely but mildly illegal one. There are signs all along the way in Spanish and English warning that there is danger and that I am trespassing on railway property, but none of the joggers and walkers, who use the path, pays any attention to them. Along this stretch of the line the tracks are only a few yards in from the edge of a cliff—there is just enough room for the footpath and a swathe of purple statice that are in bloom at the moment and clumps of elegant pampas grass. Standing at the edge of the cliff you have the delight of gulls and pelicans floating by at chest level. A few hundred feet below a mostly blue and smiling Pacific Ocean rolls onto a clean white beach, its only debris those beautiful stones I pick up and discard, and clumps of kelp. Dolphins play in these waters, and at the right time of year whales can be spotted on their way to and from their mating grounds off the coast of Mexico. There is another very Southern Californian detail in this scene: the little black figures on their long boards, waiting for the perfect wave along the line where the surf first heaves up to come rolling in. (Life on the side of the tracks—Southern California—the world of the bronzed body beautiful. Stay firm, stay beautiful, joggers, mountain bikers, walkers with dogs, couples with prams, surfers slipping down the crevices in the cliff face . . .)

The passengers on the trains headed north to Oceanside, San Clemente, San Juan Capistrano, Irvine, Santa Ana, Anaheim, Fullerton and Los Angeles—all of them neat Spanish-style stations with attractive floral features—enjoy wonderful views of the sea and coastline. It is a very different experience to that of the commuters traveling from Khayelitsha, through Nonkqubela, Nolungile, Mandalay, Philippi, Nyanga, Heideveld, Netreg, Bonteheuwel, Langa, Mutual, Ysterplaat, Paarden Eiland, to Cape Town.

A friend in Cape Town sent me a copy of a video that is shown to train drivers on this route as part of their six-month training program. It takes you from the driver's point of view, from Khayelitsha all the way into Cape Town—a fifty-minute ride through a landscape of soul-crushing squalor. At the best of times, the sandy, wind-blown Cape Flats, through which the route runs has little or no appeal; the ulcerous squatter camps of miserable shanties and pondoks, which now line the route into the mother city, are dumping grounds of hopeless human lives. Our proud slogan "The Cape of Good Hope" is a cruel misnomer for the world these people live in.

Thirty years ago, in my play *Boesman and Lena* I made a drunk and embittered Boesman describe their pondok on the mudflats of the Swartkops River as "white man's rubbish." In a paroxysm of self-hatred he goes on to say: "We pick it up, we wear it, we eat it, we're made of it now . . . we're white man's rubbish." That was the old-apartheid South Africa. This is the brave new South Africa. The people who live in these pondoks on the Cape Flats—structures every bit as flimsy and useless against the elements as the one Boesman built—can't single out the white man as the source of their rubbish anymore but, in essence, the refrain is the same: they live in a world made out of rubbish, they are the rubbish of that world.

Boesman and Lena was my first deep journey into the world of the pondok, a world that had fascinated me from my childhood when I used to accompany my mom to a butcher in a humble little Colored settlement on the outskirts of Port Elizabeth to buy black-market meat for our boarding house during the strictly rationed years of the Second World War. The nearest I can get to explaining that fascination (it is even here in Southern California when I see the simple homes of Mexican laborers) is to point to the elemental power and simplicity that the gestures and things in those lives acquire because they are so poverty-stricken, so reduced to essentials.

All my life, and I don't really know why, it has been those humble and desperate little worlds that have fired my imagination; I have studied them and tried to imagine my way into their secret life as eagerly and passionately as others do with the palaces and mansions of the mighty. What fascinates me as a writer is the way in which the destitution of these lives can sometimes invest simple things and events, even simple gestures, with huge transcendent values and resonances. When Lena breaks and shares her crust of brown bread with Outa, as they sit huddled together in the cold of the Swartkops mud-flats, it is the profound simplicity of those elements that turn that moment into a mass, a bitter celebration of her life. That crust of brown bread and mug of bitter and black tea become sacramental: "Bitter and Black" she says, "the bread should have bruises . . . it's my life Outa." A loaf of fresh white bread in the hands of a comfortable suburban housewife could never resonate in that way.

In writing that play I put together all the clues I had accumulated over the years in trying to find my way into the heart of that reality. I believe I succeeded. I revisited that play recently with a student production at the University of California in San Diego, and I can say now with conviction that there are no falsehoods in it. So, having made that imaginative journey on the mudflats, shouldn't it now be possible for me, in a similar fashion, to crawl into the pondok in the Samora Machel informal settlement that Pumla Lolwana and her three children lived? The story of South African poverty, like the story of poverty anywhere, is made up of a few very stark elements, starting with hunger and ending, as must have been the case with Pumla Lolwana, with a loss of hope. Within that terrible little span of human experience there are a few variables that can be assembled in different patterns. In her case those variables most likely included the loss of the bread-winner, her man, the father of her children. It could have been a death—those "informal settlements" are violent worlds—it could have been desertion, a man looking for his "way out" when the burden of a wife and three children became too much.

Given those possibilities, can't I now just get on with it for God's sake and give Pumla Lolwana a fictional reality and deal with her in the way that I did with Boesman and Lena? I wish I could, but the answer is again "no." Boesman and Lena wanted to live. As devastating as that night on the mud-flats had been for both of them, they are on their feet at the end, they walk away from that cold campfire and the dead black man even though it is a walk into darkness. Implicit in that walk is their will to live, an unconscious act of faith in the next day's sunrise. That is the fundamental act of faith in my life: there will be a tomorrow worth living. That is why I shied away from an earlier challenge to confront final despair.

The real Helen Martins of my play *The Road to Mecca* died in agony, caustic soda eating away her insides because she had lost faith in herself. That is not how my telling of her extraordinary story ends. I used my "liberty and license" as a storyteller to create a note of affirmation after she confronts the extinction of her creativity. But I can't play any fictional games with Pumla Lolwana. That moment when she stands on the railway lines, fiercely holding on to her children, is too final.

June 17

I was back at the tracks again this afternoon. I took a moment during my walk to stand between the tracks (when I was sure there were no trains coming) and stare along their length. I had never given them a second thought before reading Pumla Lolwana's story. But, now, those two parallel rails of steel fascinate me. There is something hypnotic and strangely menacing in the illusion of convergence as they stretched away from me. The same thing has happened to me with the trains that come charging past on my walks. They are huge double-decker leviathans with the driver's cab up at the top level. Up until now I've enjoyed them innocently as images of energy and splendor, which is how the old steam engines of my youth used to thrill me when I was growing up in Port Elizabeth. Now they also have become very unnerving, their power and momentum, their unstoppable force very frightening. The adrenaline rush that comes as they thunder past is no longer the elating thrill of my boyhood, it is fear.

One of them, a northbound Coaster, passed me on this afternoon's walk. I heard it before I saw it—a raucous blare from its horn as it left the Peñasquitos marsh and came rushing out from under the road bridge. Although I couldn't see the driver up in his cab, I gave him a wave as the train passed. I don't suppose he even noticed me.

The Cape Town commuter trains are single-deckers so those drivers do not ride as high and mighty as their American cousins. By comparison with them, the driver of the train that killed Pumla Lolwana and her children would have had a very intimate relationship with her as she stood there waiting for him. His was most probably the last human face she saw, provided, of course, that she kept her eyes open until the end. It is a thought that stops time: the two of them looking at each other, seeing each other, locked into a moment that will end the life of the mother and her children and scar his forever. The rest of my walk is a blank. The thought of those few seconds between the woman and the train driver haunted me all the way back to my writing table. I went back to the newspaper report and read:

> The train driver is receiving counseling. He is extremely traumatized, because he saw the drama play out in front of him and wasn't able to stop the train in time.

It takes three hundred meters for one of these trains traveling at a speed of seventy kilometers per hour to stop. But he most probably didn't. The instructions to the driver in the event of an accident on this line are very specific:

> If the driver is between stations he must not stop. The body will be behind him and he must continue to the next station. There he must report the incident via radio and have the police and rescue services called.

I've never really given the driver much thought, but now it occurs to me that he could possibly help me see her. If I could live through a night on the Swartkops mudflats with Boesman and Lena, then couldn't I sit in the cab with the train driver for that fatal afternoon run from Khayelitsha to Cape Town?

Unlike the mother, so emphatically identified by her name, "Pumla Lolwana," and those of her children, his very anonymity is a help. It is in fact hugely liberating. For the first time since starting to live with that newspaper story I feel a surge of energy and excitement because I realize I am free to create a fictional identity.

So here goes: His name will be "Roelf Visagie," a strong, no-nonsense, down-to-earth Afrikaans name. The railways in South Africa have always been the preserve of the Afrikaner, and if there is one South African identity I empathize with it is my mother's people. I know I've chosen a good name, because without any effort on my side "Roelf Visagie" has attracted to itself images from the life of a friend of mine in Port Elizabeth, a fishing companion of many years.

The training video that was sent me from Cape Town included interviews with and images of the drivers at the controls of the train. Their faces were those of decent but deeply troubled men who had not been able to stop the train in time—they all had their "hits"—the word used by one of them to describe those accidents. They spoke in muted tones about what it meant: "It's a life you're taking, another human being!" "You never forget the first one—no matter how many hits you have after that, you never forget the first one. Doesn't matter what it is—a cow or a dog or an old man—it's all the same, it's a life you've taken."

My Roelf Visagie would be at home in their company, drinking a cold Castle or a brandy and coke and talking about the general fuck-up of the world. For all his rough edges, my fishing friend in Port Elizabeth was also a good man; he had the same reverence for life that I saw in the faces and heard in the voices of the men in the training video.

So I decided it was going to be my Roelf Visagie's first hit—that is the dangerous side of writing, playing God with the fictional lives you've created.

He, of course, had no idea what I had in store for him that Friday afternoon. If anything, his life felt and looked particularly good as he settled down in the driver's cab for the run to Cape Town. He had a devoted wife and two lovely children (a boy and a girl), a nice house in a quiet suburb and, to complete the picture, he was a white man with a job, and a reasonably well-paid one at that, with a pension fund and medical scheme—no mean achievement in the new South Africa. But what really gave his spirits a lift when he got the signal to pull out of Khayelitsha station that Friday afternoon was his fishing prospects for the coming weekend. He was going to join two fishing buddies for a trip up the West Coast to look for steenbras. They were going to make a whole weekend of it: sleeping on the beach and returning for work early on Monday. When the train pulled into Nonkqubela station, Roelf was imagining the campfire, the lovely barbecue smell of chops and boerewors sizzling away on the coals; at Nolungile it was that electrifying moment when a fishing-reel ratchet suddenly starts screaming in the middle of the night and, still half asleep, you scramble for your rod because you know a steenbras has picked you up. The next stations were Mandalay and Philippi, and once again the train pulled in and out on time, and Roelf Visagie, with his hands on the brake and accelerator, luxuriated in the sense that his life, like his train, was under control.

The training video gives a good picture of what the drivers on this Khayelitsha–Cape Town route have to contend with. There are, of course, fences on each side of the track, which are meant obviously to keep people off, but these have been broken down or torn through in places so as to provide a shortcut from the squatter camp on one side to the camp on the other side. In the video, one constantly sees people walking next to the tracks or making suicidal dashes across them in front of the oncoming train.

With all that going on, Roelf Visagie would hardly have noticed the woman way ahead of him waiting quietly on the side. But even if he had seen her standing there—a mother with a baby on her back and two children in her arms—what of it? He must have seen at least half a dozen like her already on this run. In any case—come now, man—a mother and her children?! She's not going to go and do something stupid . . . until suddenly there she is in front of him with one of the children struggling to break loose, looking up at him, and Roelf Visagie starts to live through a few seconds that will haunt him for the rest of his life. He has his hand on the brake, his foot on the hooter, he is shouting and swearing, but it makes no difference. His life is out of control. It is over in a flash.

It wouldn't be long before a crowd would gather, pressing against the fence or crawling through its holes, for a closer look at the remains of Pumla Lolwana and her three children. And angry! Oh yes, very angry. Very loud angry voices: "Haai liewe. Here. Look at them! How many is it. A mother and three children for God's sake. Is there no bloody justice in the world? Didn't that bloody driver see her? Why didn't that fucking white man stop?"

That is why head office has ordered the drivers to just carry on to the next station in the event of an accident.

JUNE 20

Another alternative to my beach walk is along a stretch of Historic Highway 101 as it skirts the Peñasquitos marsh. This one gives me a chance to study the wonderful variety of water birds in the marsh. It is also a very schizoid experience, as it involves walking the line between two starkly contrasting worlds: stretching away from me on one side is the serene marsh, its self-contained silence broken only by the high, piping calls of curlews and sandpipers, and on the other side, just a few feet away from me as I walk along the very narrow verge, the never-ending rush and roar of traffic on the highway.

On this evening's walk, the birds were all there in the distance waiting in the muddy channels of the marsh for the incoming tide to reach them: herons and egrets, long-billed curlews and whimbrels and godwits, sandpipers and plovers. I had my binoculars focused on a great blue heron when a blue-and-white Coaster rode into its field of vision. Distance and the soft light of the evening had made it a very innocent thing of beauty; it could so easily have been a little toy train on the floor of a young boy's bedroom and not the terrible instrument a despairing soul would use to end a life.

Back at my table later I read:

> The train driver is receiving counseling. He is extremely traumatized, because he saw the drama play out in front of him and wasn't able to stop the train in time.

And then at the end of the story:

> Jaqueline van Rensburg, industrial social worker, who treats up to fifteen train drivers a month after accidents, told *Die Burger* that the drivers work under extremely difficult circumstances and feel guilty whenever anybody dies under their train. "The drivers feel very guilty because they have absolutely no control over the train."

In the training video, the drivers talk about the trauma. The advice given to them by the social worker is to talk about it, the sooner the better and to anyone who will listen.

That is the advice a sympathetic Miss Jaqueline van Rensburg gives a hesitant Mr. Visagie when he sits down awkwardly in her office for a counseling session. The likes of Roelf Visagie do not take easily to counseling, and even more so when it comes from a woman, but Miss van Rensburg knows this—he is not the first driver to come to her for help. "Whatever you are feeling, don't keep it bottled up inside you, Mr. Visagie. Talking will help you take control of the experience and put it behind you, so that you can get on with your life."

But Mr. Visagie does not find it easy. It takes a lot of patience on her side and gentle nudging before the words start to come, very haltingly at first as he clumsily feels his way into the emotional chaos inside him. She listens and watches carefully as he talks, reading signs of anger and confusion, pain and guilt. "Ja, I know, miss. I know it's not really my fault, everybody keeps telling me that—you, my wife, the other drivers—some of them have already had as many as twenty hits! Ja, that's what they call it, a 'hit.' 'It's because it's your first one, Visagie,' they say to me, 'that's why it's so hard. But give it time. You'll get over it.' I get so the hell in when people tell me that, miss. Ja. You as well. I know you are all just trying to help me, so I don't mean to be offensive, but I mean what the hell, if it's not my fault—and I don't need anybody to tell me that anymore!—then whose fault is it? Ja, why doesn't somebody try telling me that for a change instead of all this . . ." *(He leaves the sentence unfinished. Miss van Rensburg interprets the restless movement of his hands as the need for a cigarette. She tells him he can smoke if he wants to. He shakes his head.)*

"Must we point our fingers at Metrorail? Ja, why not? They don't fix up the fences on the side of the tracks where the people have broken them down. God didn't just put her down there on those tracks you know. She and her children crawled through one of those holes to get there. I've given up reporting them anymore because nobody listens. Or maybe it's the government to blame. Maybe they should take some time off from driving around in their big Mercedes Benz's and give those people decent houses to live in. You take off some time one day, miss, and go and look at those pondoks. My dog's kennel in our backyard is better than what those people is living in. And then of course there's the woman herself. Because don't think I've forgotten her. I wish I could. But, even if I could, my wife wouldn't let me because that's who she points the finger at. Ja, good old Lynette. 'She's the one who did it, Roelfie darling. Nobody dragged her and her children onto the railway lines. I don't know how a mother could do a thing like that but she did. I bet you anything you like she was drunk. So you see, liefling, it's not your fault.'

"Just like that. I got it from her again this morning. I had another bad night you see. I took the pills the doctor gave me, but the trouble is sort of . . . ag, what the hell . . . I'm sort of frightened of going to sleep, because even with the pills if I wake up it starts again, over and over—I'm looking at the tracks and then . . . I swear to God I didn't see her until suddenly there she is in front of me, waiting for me, with the children. Anyway, that is how my day started—with Lynette walking around the room, getting ready to go to her job at Pick and Pay, and I can see she's the hell in, because she also didn't get much sleep, because of me, but she is trying so hard to hide it while she tells Roelfie darling that it isn't his fault and how could a mother do a thing like that and please, liefling, go and see you doctor again and ask him for bigger pills, because these little ones isn't knocking you out . . . And while I'm sitting there on the bed watching her and listening I'm also seeing pictures of that world on the side of the tracks and it makes me naar, you know, like I want to vomit, because it's all there inside me now, ja, that for my Christmas bonus this year I got a whole rotten stinking bloody squatter camp inside me, choking me so badly I can't tell Lynette to shut the fuck up, because she doesn't know what she is talking about, she doesn't know anything. But even if she did, even if she did turn off the hair dryer and give me a chance for a change, what would I say to her? What can I say to you, miss, who finds it so easy to tell me it wasn't my fault, because she was 'looking for a way out of her troubles'? Do you know about those 'personal problems'? If I ever get back to driving you must take a ride with me one day—Khayelitsha to

Cape Town. I'll point out the beauty spots. We'll do it in winter when a good Cape storm has left that whole world under six inches of water. Then you will see, in the early morning, the mothers with their babies in their arms standing outside their pondoks, because there was no place to lie down inside. That's when you start to ask questions, miss. How long have they been standing? All night? How they going to cook food for the children?" *(Pause. This time he lights a cigarette. Ms van Rensburg revises a mental note she was going to put into his file: it's not anger she's watching, it's rage.)*

"So you see, miss, why she did it is not the problem. Ag, no, who want to live like that? Who want tomorrow if it means your children are going to be living like that? And while they're living, like getting murdered or raped or ending up with AIDS and everything else. No to hell with it. I understand why she did it. Any sensible mother would drag her kids through a hole in the fence onto those tracks if that is all they could hope for. No, miss, my problem is why the hell did she have to go and choose my train? Why didn't she wait for the guy with his twenty hits? He knows how to forget her. Instead she chooses me. No, don't shake you head! She was standing there waiting for me and I couldn't say, 'No thank you, lady, not today.' That's what people like you don't understand. There was no way out for me, miss. I couldn't swerve, I couldn't stop the fucking train. Ja, there's another joke for you if you want one. 'The controls'! 'The train driver must remain in control of the train at all times.' Bull shit! I had no more control over the train when she stood there than I did over the day I was born. If you really want to know something, miss, I'm not so sure anymore I got control over anything. And let me tell you something else: I'm not the only one. Ja. You, too! Sitting there behind your desk and looking like you're 'in control'! That driver's cab is a trap, miss, and we're all in there one way or another. We can see it coming, we head towards it at ninety kilometers an hour, but we can't swerve and the instructions from head office is, 'Don't stop, just leave the bloody mess behind you and carry on.'"

And that is as far as I go with Roelf Visagie. I could follow him out of that counseling session, into the rest of his life, the passing of time that will turn his raw wound into a scar, sit one night around a campfire on the beach with Des and Dennis, waiting for a ratchet to scream, but in doing that I would also be leaving behind the mess of the tracks between Philippi and Nyanga and I can't do that. (But, I don't know that anything is any clearer. Pumla Lolwana still stands inviolate on the tracks between Philippi and Nyanga. Instead of being in the cab with him, I feel more like one of the passengers in the coaches behind him, wondering why the train is taking so long to pull away from Nyanga station, and seeing officials running about on the platform outside and then hearing talk about a woman and three children . . .)

JUNE 24

For a change I was *in* a train, a Surfliner headed north to Los Angeles. I was on my way to watch an understudy rehearsal and to say good-bye to the wonderful cast of my play *Sorrows and Rejoicings*, which was in the last week of its run in L.A. I settled back in my comfortable business-class seat determined for once to do nothing other than look out the window and enjoy the long stretch of beautiful scenery on the route. Old habits don't break easily though, so I did have my notebook and my pen in my lap just in case. And just as well. Darwin called it his "cacoethes scribendi," his incurable itch to write. I suffer from the same complaint. It wasn't long before I had forgotten about the scenery and was scribbling away.

It had started with a delay at Oceanside station, because of work on the track. It made me wonder if there had been a parallel experience for the passengers in the coaches behind

Roelf Visagie. Had they started looking out the window, as I had just done, wondering what had gone wrong, and how long the delay would be before the train started moving again? Then, seeing officials running around outside on the platform and hearing talk about a woman and three. It was a sobering and depressing thought. It suggested that maybe all I could ever hope to be was a passenger in a train that killed a mother and her children, getting scraps of second-hand news about their death, impatient for the train to move on.

My return journey to San Diego was late at night and my notebook was again in my lap, because the itch to scratch away at a blank page was even stronger than in the morning. The cab ride from the station to the theatre had passed the county courthouse, and that had immediately brought LaShanda Crozier back into my life. Her story was carried by the *L.A. Times* ten days after I had read about Pumla Lolwana. It was then, just three days before Christmas. Her story is also a file in my computer:

Friday, December 22, 2000

HEADLINE: TROUBLED LIFE LED TO THREE DEATHS

Many people saw LaShanda Crozier's personal and financial problems, but no sign that she would throw her two daughters off a courthouse ledge, then jump.

When LaShanda Crozier pushed her two daughters to their deaths off the downtown county courthouse and followed them down, it ended a spell of economic and personal hardship, neighbors, relatives and authorities said Thursday. Crozier, twenty-seven, had talked of suffering a miscarriage that cost her a job, seeing her boyfriend lose a job, and facing eviction—the threat that brought her to the courthouse, they said.

Hours after reaching an out-of-court agreement with her landlord to gradually pay nine hundred and twenty-five dollars in back rent, Crozier pushed daughters Breanna (seven) and Joan (five) from the ninth-floor ledge and then jumped herself.

Her boyfriend, the girls' father, left the courthouse after the hearing and did not witness the deaths, authorities said. He said Thursday, "I have not come to terms with what happened to my children." He also said he was angry at Crozier, whom he described as selfish. "She should have called me at work."

Crozier owed back rent on the four-hundred-dollar-a-month apartment unit near Exposition Park that she shared with the girls and their father.

In a hallway outside Courtroom 547 on Wednesday, as they waited for the judge, Crozier and landlord Raul Almendariz tried to negotiate an agreement. He offered to allow the family to stay in their cramped, ground-floor quarters if they would start paying weekly installments of about a hundred and fifty dollars. As an alternative, Almendariz offered to let Crozier out of the lease and the back payments if she would move the family out after January first.

Almendariz said Crozier wanted to stay, even though a recent rough patch had left the couple with little money.

He said the couple told him that Crozier had spent a few days in a hospital after losing a child to a miscarriage, and that the episode cost her a job cleaning rooms at a local hotel. The boyfriend said that he had lost one of his two jobs because of the Metropolitan Transportation Authority bus drivers' strike and that his other job paid just two hundred and fifty dollars a week.

"She seemed embarrassed yesterday, about the whole situation," Almendariz said. "She didn't try to make any excuses at all. She said she would just like the opportunity to stay in the apartment and catch up on the rent." Almendariz said he agreed. Crozier signed the court papers and headed outside and into the sunshine with her boyfriend and children in tow.

Stunned family members on Thursday described Crozier as a troubled woman who had struggled economically, emotionally, and in a stormy relationship with her boyfriend. They said that in recent years she had occasionally given up custody of the two girls to an aunt, Marietta Snowden.

"She was sometimes unstable," said Snowden. "My niece was withdrawn."

Snowden also said she had been trying to retain custody of the two girls, citing her concerns about Crozier's relationship with her boyfriend, the poor living conditions at the apartment complex and Crozier's mental state. But "nobody listened, nobody listened, nobody listened," she said.

Snowden described Breanna as an outgoing tomboy who was fiercely protective of her little sister. Joan, she said, was shy and quiet, a "pretty little girl who loved to wear high-heeled sneakers."

Snowden said Breanna sensed there was something wrong with her mother and father. She said, "Auntie, I love my mama, but I don't want to stay with her."

Almendariz, like so many others who had crossed paths with Crozier, said that in recent days she had shown no signs of irrational behavior or flashes of anger or depression. There was nothing to signal that she was capable of pushing the two girls off a ledge and then jumping herself.

Witnesses later told police the two objects they saw Crozier push or throw over the ledge were the two girls. Both landed on a fourth-floor ledge and were taken to County-USC Medical Center, where they died a short time later.

Crozier landed on the ground and was pronounced dead at the scene. Los Angeles police continued to investigate the matter Thursday, and court officials reviewed their files to glean hints as to what might have prompted Crozier's actions.

Crozier was described by neighbors as friendly but quiet and somewhat guarded. She and her boyfriend kept to themselves. And they argued occasionally behind closed doors, the neighbors said.

"They had their problems," said Zelaya, but no more than anyone else in the run-down building a block west of the Los Angeles Coliseum and the USC campus. LAPD Captain Charlie Beck said the boyfriend was trying in vain Thursday to come to terms with what had happened. "He's doing awful," Beck said. "How do you even begin to understand the kind of pain that this is causing somebody?

"We will be talking to him again, see if he can put some shred of reason to this," said Beck. "But he didn't have anything he could offer . . . I don't think there is an answer for this that anyone but she will ever know."

Penelope Trickett, a developmental psychologist and professor of social work at USC, acknowledged the perplexing nature of cases in which suicidal parents choose to kill their children. "I think it has something to do with a bond between parents and kids," she said. "The feeling you are one entity, you and your children, and that if there is no hope for you, there is no hope for the children."

Landlord Almendariz said he was haunted Thursday by his last image of Crozier.

As they left the courthouse, he had just given her older daughter Breanna a twenty-dollar bill and told her to share it with her little sister as a Christmas

present. The little girl politely said, "Thank you."
And, "Yes, I will."

He said, Crozier seemed a little sad but nothing
more. "I wish I could have talked to her a little bit
more. Told her, you know, things are going to be
okay, that people have their ups and downs. I wish
there was something somebody could have done to
help," he added. "Somebody should have known how
depressed she was."

Apart from its own unique horror, what struck me about
this story, as compared with that of Pumla Lolwana, was the
wealth of personal detail and the expressions of concern and
sorrow by neighbors, relatives and authorities. What a vivid
hint there is, for example, of the characters and relationship of
Breanna and Joan, and, in contrast, the absence of any detail
about Andile, Lindani and Sesanda. I did a word count: 1266
for LaShanda Crozier, 408 for Pumla Lolwana. I have also
tried to establish if there had been any follow-up stories about
Pumla Lolwana that night possibly giving some information
about her life and circumstances, but I couldn't find any.

I have to ask myself: Is there any significance in this? Do
we South Africans put a lower value on life? Have we been so
desensitized, so numbed by our long history of violence, the
prevalence of poverty and famine in Africa, the constant bom-
bardment by the media of stories and images of starving mothers
and children on this godforsaken continent, that the death of
another mother and her three children merits only a bland and
relatively impersonal report, which gives more space to the
trauma of the train driver than to the victims of the tragedy?
I almost regret now that I know their names. It fostered the
illusion that I could somehow get to know them, understand
something about what happened on that Friday afternoon.
Anonymity would have disillusioned me of that and made
even more starkly clear the destitution of that tragic family.

At the end of *My Children! My Africa!*, just before he goes
out to confront an angry mob in what amounts to an act of
self-immolation, my Mr. M bares his soul to the young Thami
in a long monologue, which ends with this passage:

> We were on our way to a rugby match at Somerset
> East. The lorry stopped at the top of the mountain
> so that we could stretch our legs and relieve our-
> selves. It was a hard ride on the back of that lorry.
> The road hadn't been tarred yet. So there I was, ten
> years old, and sighing with relief as I aimed for the
> little bush. It was a hot day. The sun right over our
> heads . . . not a cloud in the vast blue sky. I looked
> out . . . it's very high up there at the top of the pass . . .
> and there it was, stretching away from the foot of the
> mountain, the great pan of the Karoo . . . stretch-
> ing away forever it seemed into the purple haze and
> heat of the horizon. Something grabbed my heart at
> that moment, my soul, and squeezed it until there
> were tears in my eyes. I had never seen anything so
> big, so beautiful in all my life. I went to the teacher
> who was with us and asked him: "Teacher, where
> will I come to if I start walking that way?" . . . And
> I pointed. He laughed. "Little man," he said, "that
> way is north. If you start walking that way and just
> keep on walking, and your legs don't give in, you will
> see all of Africa! Yes, Africa, little man! You will see the
> great rivers of the continent: the Vaal, the Zambesi,
> the Limpopo, the Congo, and then the mighty Nile.
> You will see the mountains: the Drakensberg, Kili-
> manjaro, Kenya and the Ruwenzori. And you will
> meet all our brothers: the little Pygmies of the for-
> ests, the proud Masai, the Watusi . . . tallest of the tall
> and the Kikuyu standing on one leg like herons in a
> pond waiting for a frog." "Has teacher seen all that?"

I asked. "No," he said. "Then how does teacher know it's there?" "Because it is all in the books and I have read the books and if you work hard in school, little man, you can do the same without worrying about your legs giving in."

He was right, Thami. *I* have seen it. It is all there in the books just as he said it was and I have made it mine. I can stand on the banks of all those great rivers, look up at the majesty of all those mountains, whenever I want to. It is a journey I have made many times. Whenever my spirit was low and I sat alone in my room, I said to myself: Walk, Anela! Walk! . . . And I imagined myself at the foot of the Wapadsberg, setting off for that horizon that called me that day forty years ago. It always worked! When I left that little room, I walked back into the world a proud man, because I was an African and all the splendor was my birthright.

(Pause) I don't want to make that journey again, Thami. There is someone waiting for me now at the end of it who has made a mockery of all my visions of splendor. He has in his arms my real birthright. I saw him on the television in the Reverend Mbopa's lounge. An Ethiopian tribesman, and he was carrying the body of a little child that had died of hunger in the famine . . . a small bundle carelessly wrapped in a few rags. I couldn't tell how old the man was. The lines of despair and starvation on his face made him look as old as Africa itself.

He held that little bundle very lightly as he shuffled along to a mass grave, and when he reached it, he didn't have the strength to kneel and lay it down gently . . . He just opened his arms and let it fall. I was very upset when the program ended. Nobody had thought to tell us his name and whether he was the child's

father, or grandfather, or uncle. And the same for the
baby! Didn't it have a name? How dare you show me
one of our children being thrown away and not tell
me its name! I demand to know who is in that bundle!

(Pause) Not knowing their names doesn't matter anymore. They are more than just themselves. The tribesman and dead child do duty for all of us, Thami. Every
African soul is either carrying that bundle or in it.

What is wrong with this world that it wants to
waste you all like that . . . my children . . . my Africa!

Standing there on the railway line between Philippi and
Nyanga, with her children in her arms, Pumla Lolwana joins
that Ethiopian tribesman with a matching and terrifying loneliness; a Stabat Mater Dolorosa without a redeeming Christ
on the cross.

JUNE 27

It is either late at night/very early in the morning and I am
lying awake in bed. I resist looking at the luminous dial of my
wristwatch because I know that that will only make going back
to sleep more difficult. But for once I am not fretting about
my insomnia, I am listening to a freight train—it is heading
south—I can both hear and feel the vibrations of passing train
traffic in my bedroom. This is a long one and I try to count
the individual trucks as they trundle heavily over the bridge in
the marsh, but after a few seconds I loose count because whenever I hear a passing train these days I always end up thinking
about Pumla Lolwana. How close was her pondok to the railway line? Did she lie awake at night listening to passing trains?
Is that how she got the idea? Playing back the images I have of
her final moments, there is one which I surprisingly (and for
reasons that elude me) have a dark sympathy with, almost an

understanding: It is the moment when Sesanda tried to escape and she pulled him back and held on to him fiercely as the train sped closer. *"If you live, so must I, but I can't, I cant . . ."*

And that last walk of hers with the children. It would have been dramatic to picture it in pouring rain, mother and children drenched to the skin, but that is not the case. That last walk was in bright and mild sunshine, with just a gentle breeze blowing and hardly a cloud in the sky—I have the weather report for that day.

Women walking. Pumla Lolwana is not the only powerful and virtually nameless presence in my life. She has sisters. My notebooks record a few other destitute women who have walked across my path leaving their shadows on my work. In August 1965, I made this entry about a life I gave to an old African woman:

We picked her up about ten miles outside Cradock. She was carrying all her worldly possessions in a bundle on her head and in an old shopping bag. I'd guess about seventy years old. Cleft palate. A very hot day.

Her story was that she had been chased off a farm after her husband's death about three days previously. She was walking to another farm where she had a friend. Later on she told us that she had nine children but didn't know where they were. She thought a few of them were in P.E.

After driving about fifteen miles, it became obvious that she would never have reached her destination on foot that day. We asked her about this, and she said she knew it, and would have slept in one of the storm-water drains.

She cried frequently. The first time was when I took the bundle (it was very heavy) off her head and put it in the boot and she realized she was going to get a lift. She told May she couldn't believe it: "It was like a dream." Then in the car, telling her story, she cried again. May comforted her. Finally, when we reached the gate where she wanted to get off and I gave her two of the three shillings left in my pocket, she cried again. I put the bundle on her head. May carried the shopping bag down an embankment to the gate and set her on her way. My last image of her is the thin, scrawny ankles between her old shoes and the edge of her old skirt, trudging away into the bush. I suppose she stopped to cry a little and then went on, cried again later and went on, went on and on.

Barney—about her bundle: "She still has a use for the things in her life." And just her life; still using it—feeding it, sleeping it, washing it.

Her bundle consisted of one of those heavy three-legged iron pots, a blanket and an old zinc bath full of other odds and ends—all this tied together with a dirty piece of flaxen twine. In the old shopping bag I spotted a bottle of tomato sauce and Barney spotted a packet of OMO [laundry powder].

Finally only this to say: that in that cruel walk under the blazing sun, walking from all of her life (which she didn't have on her head), facing the prospect of a bitter Karoo night in a drainpipe, in this walk there was no defeat—there was pain, and great suffering, but no defeat.

In 1968 this entry:

Another Colored woman who might have been a model for my Lena. Lived somewhere in the bush along the Glendore Road. Worked for us for a short period about two years ago. Sense of appalling physical and spiritual destitution, of servility. Did the housework without a word or sound, without the slightest flicker of her "self." For some reason left us after about two months. Then some time later came back to see if we had any work. A stiflingly hot day . . . Berg wind blowing. In the course of the few words I had with her she seemed to be in an even more desperate condition than when we had last seen her (not so much physically, though that was still there, but poverty is poverty, and at its worst there are no grades), it was a sense of her disorientation, almost derangement, of only a fraction of herself committed to and involved in the world around her. After telling the woman we had no work, she left us to try a few other houses.

An hour or so later, the heat even more fierce by then, I left the house with snorkel and mask to do some skin-diving in the gullies. I would not have moved out into that sun if it hadn't been for the prospect of the wet cool sea. I looked back at one point, just before going over the edge of the headland and down to the rocks, and saw the woman, empty-handed and obviously unsuccessful in her search for work, starting up the hill on her way back to Glendore.

That hill, the sun, the long walk. Possibly even a walk that Lena has not yet made . . . but will one day in the time that still lies ahead of her when she walks away with Boesman at the end of the play; a walk beyond the moment of rebellion—that possibility past, even forgotten—a walk beyond all the battles, the refusals, even tears. Surrender. Defeat. A walk into the ignominy of silence, the world's silence and blindness, burdened now as never before by Lena's unanswerable little words: "Why?" "How?" "Who?"

And a few years later there was Patience—"My English name is Patience"—with her baby on her back on the road outside Graaff-Reinet:

I nearly didn't stop for her. She didn't signal that she wanted a lift or anything like that. Didn't even look up when I passed . . . I was watching her in the rear-view mirror. Maybe that's what told me there was a long walk ahead of her . . . the way she had her head down and just kept on walking. And then the baby on her back. It was hot out there, hot and dry, and a lot of empty space . . . There wasn't a farmhouse in sight. She looked very small and unimportant in the middle of all that. Anyway, I stopped and reversed and offered her a lift. Not very graciously. I was in a hurry and wanted to get to the village before it got dark. She got in, and after a few miles we started talking. Her English wasn't very good, but when I finally got around to understanding what she was trying to tell me it added up to another typical South African story. Her husband, a farm laborer, had died recently, and no sooner had they buried him when the baas told her to pack up and leave the farm. So there she was . . . on her way to the Cradock district, where she hoped to find a few distant relatives and a place to live. About my age. The baby couldn't have been more than a few months old. All she had with her was one of those plastic shopping bags they put your groceries in at supermarkets. I saw a pair of old slippers. She was barefoot.

So now it is Pumla walking. Was it purposeful? Heading straight to the tracks, her mind made up, very clear about what she was going to do? Holding the hands of her small children, crooning softly to the baby on her back, hoping the infant would stay asleep until the end? No. I reject that scenario. Lying there in the dark, it surprises me to realize that even though all I have and know about Pumla Lolwana is her name and those of her children, I now have such a strong sense of her dark presence that I feel I have the authority to accept or reject possible scenarios concerning her. I see instead a random drift through that wasteland of lives called the Samora Machel informal settlement in search of something—a friend or a relative or the man, husband or boyfriend, who didn't come home with his pay-packet the night before, a search for anything or anybody that could be a source of hope, give her a reason to live. She never found it and when she finally paused to rest, with little Sesanda asking: *"Where are we going, Mommy? What's wrong, Mommy?"* she was at the side of the railway tracks and a train was coming.

Women walking. Always women. Is the reason for that as simple as that early childhood memory I have of my mother (possibly the earliest)? She was trudging heavily and wearily up the hill to where we lived and I had run to meet her. She was dispirited and depressed after a bad day in the bakery where she worked. It was a terrible shock to see her like that. She was the central and most important presence in my life. Seeing her defeated meant that my whole world was in danger of collapsing.

In the years that followed, I saw my mother, metaphorically speaking, trudging up that hill many times. Her life was one long struggle or survival—for herself and her family. But she—and because of her, Lena and Milly and Hester and Miss Helen and all the other women in my work, who draw their inspiration from my mother—were never defeated, and that is the cardinal difference. Pumla Lolwana was. And it is that difference, which maybe now defeats me, and makes Pumla Lolwana the dark mystery she will always be for me. There was no hope left.

Lying there in the dark, I realize that the freight train has long since passed and all is silent once again, that soft sibilant silence of a sleeping suburban world. I can't even hear the surf, which is only a few hundred yards away from where I lie in my bed.

June 29

I read:

> By Monday night nobody had claimed the bodies of
> the mother and her three children from the Salt River
> mortuary.

Nobody ever did. Pumla Lolwana's story ends in a sandy
windblown cemetery on the Cape Flats where she and her
children were given a pauper's burial. I realize suddenly that
there is another personal connection here, this one going back
all of fifty years to London where my wife Sheila and I are in
the Everyman's Cinema in Hampstead watching *The Burmese
Harp*. It is a beautiful film with its unforgettable central image
of a Japanese Buddhist monk traveling through a war-ravaged
Burmese landscape, burying the bodies of fellow countrymen
killed in battle and left to rot on the battlefields. At the time
I didn't appreciate how deep an impression this film made on
me. I certainly recognized it as a deeply religious work of art,
but that is as far as it went. Now I see it as possibly the genesis
of a theme—burying the dead—which has been there in my
work from fairly early on and very much so in recent years.

The story of Antigone captured my imagination at a very
early age. It is hard to think of a story that could have been
more urgently needed in the apartheid South Africa in which
I grew up than that of the young girl defying the laws of the
state because the unwritten laws of her conscience demanded
that she bury her brother. It was inevitable that sooner or
later Serpent Players—the black drama group I started in Port
Elizabeth—would take on Sophocles' magnificent play. The
story of that one lone voice raised in protest against what she
considered an unjust law struck to the heart of every member
of the group.

This production had long-term consequences, leading to the arrest of a member of the group, who then staged a two-character version of the play—just Creon and Antigone—on Robben Island, which in turn led to the writing of *The Island*. Some years later a photograph of two South African soldiers dumping the bodies of dead Swapo fighters in a mass grave in South West Africa led to the writing of *Playland*. A few years after that, a newspaper item about unclaimed bodies in a police mortuary in the then Transvaal—victims of a black-on-black political massacre—resulted in the story of Lukas Jantjies, a Colored man just a few years older than myself, who is haunted by the thought of those unclaimed bodies.

And now those of Pumla Lolwana and her three children in the Salt River mortuary. Is that what hooked me when I first read the story? Was that possibly the reason why I couldn't pass it over, consign to oblivion as, in fact, time is trying to do to it? Is that why she has haunted me? Must I claim her? Yes, I want to do that. As I sit at my table this morning the deepest impulse in my heart is to claim them as mine. And why not! Nobody else wanted them. Maybe that is what I've been trying to do these past weeks at this table, claim her and her children, and bury them in the blank pages of this notebook. With that thought I feel that something has changed inside me in much the same way as the haunting stopped for Lukas Jantjies when he realized he had to bury the dead.

Every Sunday night here in Southern California I drive inland for two hours to Metta, a Thai Buddhist forest monastery in an isolated valley, to join the abbot and his five monks for the evening chanting and meditation. I center my very simple Buddhist practice around one section of the chanting:

All human beings are the owners of their actions, heir to their actions, born of their actions, related through their actions and live dependent on their actions. Whatever they do, for good or for evil, to that will they fall heir.

On my last visit, I told the abbot about Pumla Lolwana and her children, and asked him if there was a prayer I could say or something I could do for the four of them. He suggested that I should dedicate whatever merit I earned from my next meditation, to them. How do I do that, I asked? Say it, he said. Simply say aloud or to yourself: "I dedicate whatever merit to . . ."

I started by saying their names aloud, because apart from a few impersonal facts, that is all I have of them:

Pumla Lolwana . . . thirty-five years old
Sesanda Lolwana . . . five years old
Andile Lolwana . . . three years old
Lindani Lolwana . . . two years old

Those four names have become infinitely precious to me. For all I know, here where I am, ten thousand miles away from where they died, I might be the only person left still thinking and saying them. They tell their own story—starting with those of the two boys, a simple story that speaks of a family that had grown stronger with each of their births; then came little Lindani, the daughter the mother had prayed and waited for. And then, of course, the mother herself: Pumla . . . which in Xhosa means to rest, to sleep, to find peace.

I was wrong when I started out to think that I needed to "understand" what happened that Friday afternoon on the tracks between Philippi and Nyanga. That isn't why Pumla Lolwana stopped my life. It wasn't either to witness—that thin newspaper report did all that could be done by those who weren't there, didn't see it. I had to claim her, for myself. Now, having done that, I have a sense as powerful as the one that made me stop a few weeks ago—I can now move on.

JUNE 30

I ended the day with a sunset walk next to the tracks. It was a quiet one. No trains passed. In spite of a very dry season, the statice are still putting on a show. Out at sea there were a few distant pools of silvery light when sunshine broke through a bank of clouds and spilt onto the water. Also, a cool and very refreshing breeze. I looked at my wristwatch: eight P.M. here, four A.M. in the morning in Cape Town. When I got back to my table I went online to get Cape Town's weather forecast: it promised a cloudless, sunny day with light winds and a maximum temperature of nineteen degrees Celsius. The people of the Samora Machel squatter camp were in for a beautiful, mild winter's day.

HAROLD ATHOL LANIGAN Fugard was born on June 11, 1932, in Middelburg, Great Karoo, Cape Province, South Africa. He has written close to fifty plays, as well as four books and several screenplays. His plays include *Blood Knot* (1961); *Boesman and Lena* (1969); *"Master Harold" . . . and the boys* (1982); *The Road to Mecca* (1984) and *My Children! My Africa!* (1989). Many of his works were turned into films: *Tsotsi*, based on his 1980 novel, won the 2005 Academy Award, for best foreign language film. His work spans the period of apartheid in South Africa (imposed in 1948), through the first democratic elections (April 27, 1994), when Nelson Mandela became president, and into the aftermath of the present day. South Africa's best-known playwright, and one of the most performed playwrights in the world, at eighty, Fugard continues to direct and write plays.

CPSIA information can be obtained
at www.ICGtesting.com
Printed in the USA
JSHW061232200822
29445JS00002B/1